Rock 'n' Roll

Tom Stoppard's other work includes *Rosencrantz and Guildenstern Are Dead*, *The Real Inspector Hound*, *Jumpers*, *Travesties*, *Night and Day*, *Every Good Boy Deserves Favour* (with André Previn), *After Magritte*, *Dirty Linen*, *The Real Thing*, *Hapgood*, *Arcadia*, *Indian Ink*, *The Invention of Love* and the trilogy *The Coast of Utopia*. His radio plays include: *If You're Glad I'll Be Frank*, *Albert's Bridge*, *Where Are They Now?*, *Artist Descending a Staircase*, *The Dog It Was That Died* and *In the Native State*. Work for television includes *Professional Foul* and *Squaring the Circle*. His film credits include *Empire of the Sun*, *Rosencrantz and Guildenstern Are Dead*, which he also directed, *Shakespeare in Love* (with Marc Norman) and *Enigma*.

TOM STOPPARD

Rock 'n' Roll

faber and faber

This revised edition first published in 2006
by Faber and Faber Limited
Bloomsbury House, 74-77 Great Russell St, London WC1B 3DA

Reprinted with further revisions 2008

Typeset by Country Setting, Kingsdown, Kent CT14 8ES
Printed and bound by CPI Group (UK) Ltd., Croydon, CR0 4YY

A CIP record for this book
is available from the British Library

ISBN 978–0–571–24242–9

4 6 8 10 9 7 5 3

For Václav Havel

Acknowledgements

My first debt is to Václav Havel, whose essays, commentaries and letters from 1965 to 1990 and beyond were not just indispensable to the play but a continual inspiration in the writing. I am indebted, too, to Paul Wilson and Jaroslav Riedel for many helpful conversations about the Plastic People of the Universe and the rock 'n' roll scene in Czechoslovakia. My thanks are due to David Gilmour, Tim Willis, Martin Deeson, Trevor Griffiths, Eric Hobsbawm, David West, Peter Jones and many others who allowed me to bother them with my questions.

T.S.

Introduction

In the first draft of *Rock 'n' Roll* Jan was called Tomas, my given name which, I suppose, is still my name. My surname was legally changed when I was, like Jan, unexpectedly 'a little English schoolboy'.

This is not to say that the parallels between Jan's life and mine go very far. He was born where I was born, in Zlin, and left Czechoslovakia for the same reason (Hitler) at much the same time. But Jan came directly to England as a baby, and returned to Czechoslovakia in 1948, two years after I arrived in England having spent the war years in the Far East.

The two-year overlap was the basis of my identification with Jan, and why I started off by calling him Tomas. His love of England and of English ways, his memories of his mother baking *buchty*, and his nostalgia for his last summer and winter as an English schoolboy are mine.

If that had been the whole play (or part of a play I'd often thought about writing, an autobiography in a parallel world where I returned 'home' after the war), Tomas would have been a good name for the protagonist. But with *Rock 'n' Roll* the self-reference became too loose, and, for a different reason, misleading, too, because I also had in mind another Tomas altogether, the Tomas of Milan Kundera's novel *The Unbearable Lightness of Being*.

In that book there is a scene where Tomas refuses to sign a petition on behalf of political prisoners gaoled by Husák's 'government of normalisation', which followed the invasion by the Warsaw Pact armies. In the play, when Jan is asked to sign what is essentially the same petition at the same juncture, his response is taken directly from Kundera's Tomas, in distillation:

> **Jan** No, I won't sign it. First because it won't help Hubl and the others, but mainly because helping them is not its real purpose. Its real purpose is to let Ferdinand and his friends feel they're not absolutely pointless. It's just moral exhibitionism . . . All they're doing is exploiting the prisoners' misfortune to draw attention to themselves. If they're so concerned for the families they should go and do something useful for the families, instead of – for all they know – making things worse for the prisoners.

However, the primary source for this is not *The Unbearable Lightness of Being* but a polemical exchange years earlier between Kundera and Václav Havel, which prefigured not only Tomas's (and now Jan's) accusation of 'moral exhibitionism' but also Jan's half of his argument with his activist friend Ferdinand, where Jan insists that the Prague Spring was by no means 'defeated' by the Russian invasion. 'The new politics' had 'survived this terrible conflict', Kundera wrote at the time. 'It retreated, yes, but it did not disintegrate, it did not collapse.' Intellectual life had not been shackled. The police state had not 'renewed itself'.

Kundera's essay – titled 'Czech Destiny', or perhaps 'The Czech Lot' – was published in December 1968, four months after the invasion. The fact that it was published at all may have been thought to support its argument –

> **Jan** For once this country found the best in itself. We've been done over by big powerful nations for hundreds of years but this time we refused our destiny.

But Havel was having none of it. Disaster was not a moral victory, and, as for 'destiny', Havel wrote, Kundera was indulging in a mystical self-deception and refusing to face plain fact. In the play, Ferdinand is briefer and ruder – 'It's not destiny, you moron, it's the neighbours worrying about *their* slaves revolting if we get away with it.'

Kundera fired back a few months later ('moral exhibitionism'), and it should be said that both writers would have cause for complaint if the play purported to deploy their arguments fairly. Dramatists become essayists at their peril. The play does not take account of Havel's Parthian shot in an interview years later:

> All those who did not sign or who withdrew their signatures argued in ways similar to Tomas in Kundera's novel . . . Naturally the president [Husák] did not grant an amnesty, and so Jaroslav Sabata, Milan Hubl and others went on languishing in prison, while the beauty of our characters was illuminated. It would seem, therefore, that history proved our critics to be right. But was that really the case? I would say not. When the prisoners began to come back after their years in prison, they all said that the petition had given them a great deal of satisfaction. Because of it, they felt that their stay in prison had a meaning: it helped renew the broken solidarity . . . But it had a far deeper significance as well: it marked the beginning of a process in which people's civic backbone began to straighten again. This was a forerunner to Charter 77 . . .

The scene between Ferdinand and Jan when Ferdinand has just had a spell in prison is again in debt to a robust exchange of essays, this time between Havel and the novelist Ludvik Vaculík in December and January 1978/9. I moved the conversation forward to 1975 (otherwise it would have had to occur in the interval);

which is not quite fair to 'Notes on Courage' by Vaculík, because the stress for dissident intellectuals must have been worse after the watershed of Charter 77. Vaculík, like Jan, says that he's afraid of prison. He is looking for a 'decent middle ground', and, like Jan, sees himself as a 'normal person'. 'Normal people are not "heroes".' Echoing Vaculík, Jan complains to Ferdinand that heroism isn't honest work, the kind that keeps the world going round: 'It offends normal people and frightens them. It seems to be about some private argument the heroes are having with the government on our behalf, and we never asked you.' Heroic acts didn't spring from people's beliefs – 'I believe the same as you do' – they sprang from character and 'It's not the action of a friend to point out that your character is more heroic than mine.'

A related point was made in another *samizdat* essay, by Petr Pithart, which made its appearance at almost the same time. This spoke for a 'passive majority' of like-believers against an 'active minority' of 'self-anointed activists'. This minority, said Pithart, alluding to the Charter 'spokesmen', inevitably became ever more absorbed in its internal problems and quarrels and lost touch with the concerns of the majority.

Havel, again in *samizdat* (the days of open publication were long past), replied to both Vaculík and Pithart as he had to Kundera ten years before, unrepentantly. All of these deeply pondered, deeply felt exchanges between intellectuals and friends living under pressures hardly imaginable by writers in the West would support a whole play of political and moral philosophy. But that play is not *Rock 'n' Roll*.

If it were, if the playwright didn't have other fish to fry in his allotted time, it would have been Ferdinand's role to speak for Havel. That's why I named him Ferdinand.

In the first draft, Ferdinand had a surname, Vanek. 'Ferdinand Vanek' is the name of a character in three of Havel's plays – *Audience*, *Private View* and *Protest* – where he stands in for the author. Vanek is a banned playwright. In *Audience* he is employed in a brewery, just as Havel was in 1974.

I had worked out that, in my play, Tomas (later Jan) would need a foil who would be taking Havel's viewpoint in the dialectic. All of a sudden I had the inspiration of borrowing 'Ferdinand Vanek' for the role. A moment later, in my delight at this idea, I thought of placing one of my Vanek–Tomas scenes in that very brewery and even, perhaps, including the brewmaster who was the second character in *Audience*.

During a visit to Prague I had the opportunity to ask Havel's permission to use his character in my unwritten play. He gave it without demur. He said it would be an honour. He didn't seem especially surprised by my brilliantly original notion. Not until I came to be writing these notes did I discover that I was at last count the fourth author to put 'Ferdinand Vanek' into his own play.

Not only that, I had met two of the other three (as well as Havel) when I first went to Prague in 1977. Pavel Landovsky, an actor, was the first to have the idea. His 'Vanek' trod the boards in Germany in a full-length play in 1976. (The play failed, Landovsky says, because the title, *Sanitation Night*, had been translated as *Closed for Disinfection*, and this fatal phrase turned away anyone disposed to enter the theatre.) Two years later, the playwright and novelist Pavel Kohout wrote his own Vanek play, which was put on the following year in Vienna with Havel's third Vanek play, *Protest*, in a double-bill. The third author, Jiří Dienstbier, not only wrote a Vanek play, he included the Brewmaster, too. I had been trumped three times over before I had played my card. (What made it all the more piquant was that I had put Kohout into a play of mine, *Dogg's Hamlet, Cahoot's Macbeth*, which was staged in London in the same month Kohout's first Vanek play – he wrote two more – was receiving its premiere in Vienna.)

By the time I caught up on all this,[*] Ferdinand had lost his surname anyway. I didn't know, when I began, that in the second half of my play it would be Jan, and not Ferdinand, who would be Havel's spirit. I ought to have realised that I wouldn't be able to – or wish to – sustain Jan as a cautious dissenter from dissent. Whether or not Tomas (that is, I myself) would have signed the Charter and gone jobless or even to gaol is something I'll never know, but if, in my parallel biography, I had kept my head below the parapet, it would have been out of fear and timidity, not out of disagreement with Havel's philosophical and political writing.

Jan, at any rate, changes. He no longer takes his cues from Kundera or Vaculík, or from the bohemian underground which deprecated the 'official opposition' of banned writers, artists and intellectuals ('a bunch of tossers'). In the second act, he takes over Vanek's mantle from Ferdinand, at least by implication. In temperament Vanek could not really be either a Ferdinand or a Jan; his nature is too polite and reticent. But Jan now takes his cues from Havel.

The most important sources for the 'Czech arguments' in this play are the essays, articles and letters written by Havel between 1968 and the 1990s. I'd had most of them on my shelves since publication but had been lazy about

[*] All the information about the Vanek plays comes from Carol Rocamora's careful and comprehensive book about Havel's life and work, *Acts of Courage* (Smith and Kraus, 2004), which, absurdly, I never got round to reading earlier because I was too involved in my play.

reading them properly. (An exception was a speech, 'Politics and Conscience', read out *in absentia* in Toulouse when Havel was awarded an honorary doctorate from that university but prevented from travelling there to receive it. At his request I represented him on that occasion.) When I did read them all within the space of a few weeks in 2004 I was left with an overwhelming sense of humility and pride in having a friend of such bravery, humanity and clear-sighted moral intelligence; who, moreover, as was clear even in translation, was as complex and subtle in his long paragraphs as he was adroit in his dialogues. The open letter titled 'Dear Dr Husák' (1975) and the long essay, ninety pages in my edition, called 'The Power of the Powerless' (1978) were influential in their own time and place, but transcend both and will continue to be important wherever 'living in truth' requires not merely conscience but courage.*

Rock 'n' Roll manages to allude to only a tiny fraction of Havel's writing. The Toulouse speech by itself is a mine of timely reminders of the need to put morality above politics, and nature above scientific triumphalism; to return life to its human scale, and language to its human meaning; to recognise that socialism and capitalism in their selfish forms are different routes to global totalitarianism. A later essay, 'Stories and Totalitarianism' (1987), provides Jan with his dialogue about there being 'no stories in Czechoslovakia . . . We aim for inertia. We mass-produce banality'; and about pseudo-history in pseudo-newspapers. The assertion that

* Much of Havel's prose writing, notably 'The Power of the Powerless' (in *Open Letters*, Faber and Faber, 1991) and *Letters to Olga* (Faber and Faber, 1988), has been translated by Paul Wilson, who made translations for me of the exchanges between Havel and Kundera, Vaculík and Pithart referred to earlier. Wilson, a Canadian, has the further distinction of having been a member of the rock band Plastic People of the Universe between 1970 and 1972 (vocals and rhythm guitar).

Czechoslovakia's need is deeper than a return to Western democracy is one of a hundred striking moments in 'The Power of the Powerless'. It is in the same essay that Havel observes that 'living in truth' could be any means by anyone who rebels against being manipulated by the Communist regime: it could be attending a rock concert.

*

Even if *Rock 'n' Roll* were entirely about the Czech experience between the Prague Spring and the Velvet Revolution, it could only hope to be a diagram. Yet, a diagram can pick out lines of force which may be faint or dotted on the intricate map of history that takes in all accounts. *Rock 'n' Roll* crystalised around one short essay by Havel, 'The Trial' (1976), and a few pages in a book-length interview from 1985. (Havel worked on the transcript, which became the first *samizdat* book to be legally published in post-Communist Czechoslovakia. Translated by Paul Wilson under the title *Disturbing the Peace*, it was published in England by Faber and Faber in 1990.)

The interviewer, Karel Hvizdala, asked about the origin of Charter 77. Havel's reply began like this:

> For me personally, it all began sometime in January or February 1976. I was at Hradecek, alone, there was snow everywhere, a night blizzard was raging outside. I was writing something, and suddenly there was a pounding on the door, I opened it, and there stood a friend of mine, whom I don't wish to name, half-frozen and covered with snow. We spent the night discussing things over a bottle of cognac he'd brought with him. Almost as an aside, this friend suggested that I meet Ivan Jirous . . . I already knew Jirous; I'd met him about twice in the late 1960s but I hadn't seen him since then. Occasionally I would hear wild and, as I discovered later, quite distorted stories about the

group of people that had gathered round him, which he called the underground, and about the Plastic People of the Universe, a nonconformist rock group that was at the centre of this society; Jirous was their artistic director.

Havel goes on to explain that Jirous's opinion of him 'was not exactly flattering either: he apparently saw me as a member of the official, and officially tolerated, opposition – in other words, a member of the establishment'.

Havel and Jirous met in Prague a month later: 'His hair was down to his shoulders, other long-haired people would come and go, and he talked and talked and told me how things were.'

Jirous played Havel songs by the Plastic People on an old tape-recorder. 'There was disturbing magic in the music, and a kind of inner warning. Here was something serious and genuine . . . Suddenly I realised that, regardless of how many vulgar words these people used or how long their hair was, truth was on their side; . . . in their music was an experience of metaphysical sorrow and a longing for salvation.'

Jirous and Havel went to a pub and talked through the night. It was arranged that Havel would go to their next 'secret' concert in two weeks' time, but before that happened Jirous and the band were arrested, along with other members of the underground.

Havel set about getting support for the prisoners, but among the people who might have helped almost no one knew them, and those who did tended to think of them as layabouts, hooligans, drug addicts. They were at first inclined to see the case as a criminal affair. But for Havel it was 'an attack by the totalitarian system on life itself, on the very essence of human freedom and integrity'.

Somewhat to his surprise, his contacts quickly got the point: the 'criminals' were simply young people who wanted to live in harmony with themselves, and to express themselves in a truthful way. If this judicial attack went unchallenged, the regime could well start locking up anyone who thought and expressed himself independently, even in private.

The Plastic People affair became a *cause célèbre*. The regime backtracked, and started releasing most of those arrested. Ultimately, Jirous and three others came to trial in Prague in September 1976. Havel attended the trial and wrote about it: this was the other text – 'The Trial' – which was a focal point in the writing of *Rock 'n' Roll*.

Milan Hlavsa, who died in 2001, formed the Plastic People of the Universe (he took the name from a song by the American rock musician Frank Zappa) in September 1968 when he was nineteen. The fact that the Russian invasion of Czechoslovakia had occurred in August was not immediately relevant: 'We just loved rock 'n' roll and wanted to be famous.' The occupation by the Warsaw Pact armies was background, 'the harsh reality', but 'rock 'n' roll wasn't just music to us, it was kind of life itself'. Hlavsa made the point more than once in his interviews. The band was not interested in bringing down Communism, only in finding a free space for itself inside the Communist society.

But of course there was no such space, and the story that *Rock 'n' Roll* is telling is that, in the logic of Communism, what the band wasn't interested in and what the band wanted could not in the end be separated. There were dozens of rock bands in Prague, and elsewhere in Czechoslovakia who were 'not interested in bringing down Communism', and they prospered according to their lights, in some cases because the ground rules entailed no compromises on their part, in other cases because the ground rules did. The Plastics were among a small number of musicians and artists who wouldn't compromise at all, so the space for their music and for 'life itself' became harder and harder to find until it was eradicated.

The Plastic People of the Universe did not bring down Communism, of course. After the trial, Husák strengthened his grip on the country until the end came thirteen years later. What could not be separated were disengagement and dissidence. In the play Jan tells a British journalist, 'Actually, the Plastics is not about dissidents'. The reporter replies, 'It's about dissidents. Trust me.' And he's right. The rock 'n' roll underground, as Jirous said, was an attack on the official culture of Communist Czechoslovakia, and in case he didn't get the point, the regime sent him to gaol four times during those twenty years: culture is politics.

Jirous is one of the most interesting and least known personalities in the story of the Czechoslovak Socialist Republic between the Prague Spring and the Velvet Revolution. He is not a musician; he was trained as an art historian. He joined up with the Plastic People in April 1969 in the brief period before they lost their licence, and he took over as their impresario and artistic director on the long bumpy road from professional status to amateur to outcast. It was his own integrity which he made the distinguishing attribute of the band, and he managed to see their travails as an enviable fate compared with the 'underground' in the West,

> where . . . some of those who gained recognition and fame came into contact with official culture . . . which enthusiastically accepted them and swallowed them up, as it accepts and swallows up new cars, new fashions or anything else. In Bohemia the situation is essentially different, and far better than in the West,

because we live in an atmosphere of complete agreement: the first [official] culture doesn't want us, and we don't want anything to do with the first culture. This eliminates the temptation that for everyone, even the strongest artist, is the seed of destruction: the desire for recognition, success, winning prizes and titles, and last but not least, the material security which follows.

This comes from Jirous's 'Report on the Third Czech Musical Revival', written in February 1975, a year before he met Havel. It has an epigraph which might have been written by Havel: 'There is only one way for the people – to free themselves by their own efforts. Nothing must be used that would do it for them . . . Cast away fear! Don't be afraid of commotion.' In fact, it was written by Mao Tse-Tung; a long stretch. In *Rock 'n' Roll*, Max the Marxist philosopher says that he is 'down to one belief, that between theory and practice there's a decent fit – not perfect but decent'. The equivalence of theory and practice is nowhere harder to achieve than in 'living in truth' in a society which lies to itself. In the Czechoslovakia of 1968 to 1990 a rock 'n' roll band came as close as anyone.

Author's Notes

THE SETTING

'Cambridge' always refers to part of the interior and part of the garden of a family house in (probably) a leafy suburb of the city: not a modern house. It may be desirable to vary the proportion between the visible interior and the visible garden.

'Prague' mostly refers to the living room of Jan's very modest apartment, but there are important exceptions, including some exteriors. Regarding the apartment, Jan's record collection and the record player are obviously important, and a table with two chairs is probably the minimum necessary furniture. A 'bathroom/lavatory entrance', a 'bedroom entrance' and an entry door are all implied, possibly in view.

RECORDED MUSIC

. . . is subject to permissions. It is not the intention that the songs between the scenes be played complete, but as fragments (thirty to sixty seconds) breaking off arbitrarily when the next scene is ready to go. ('Vera' in Act Two is an exception.) In the first production of *Rock 'n' Roll* 'sleeve notes' for each recording were projected during the scene changes. This is strongly recommended: they kept the show going during the blackouts.

'GOLDEN HAIR'

'Golden Hair' as recorded by Syd Barrett is based on a poem by James Joyce from *Chamber Music* (in *Poems and Shorter Writings*, Faber and Faber). Barrett's lyrics, however, do not conform to Joyce's poem (where

'Goldenhair' is one word and where the phrase 'in the midnight air' does not occur). I am grateful to the James Joyce Estate for its tolerance in this matter.

SCENE CHANGES

I use the phrase 'smash cut' to mean that all the cues for sound and light are called as one cue, so that one state (e.g., music in blackout) jumps into a completed state (e.g., silence and daylight) without fades or builds. Before each scene, if the year changes, the appropriate date is projected.

CZECH DIALOGUE

Since this is a reading copy of *Rock 'n' Roll* for English-speakers, I have not included dialogue in Czech. Where Czech is spoken, the burden of the dialogue is made clear to the reader. I do not know Czech myself, so I have no qualms about actors and directors making their own arrangements to supply the utterance, which in any case is half-buried by hubbub (as at the beginning of the lunch party) or music (bar room).

ACCENTS

Czech characters speaking 'Czech' to each other do so without accents. Czech characters speaking English speak with a 'Czech accent'.

MEN'S HAIR

. . . is a problem. In Act One, Jan and Ferdinand should start off with moderately long hair which gets, in Jan's case, very long until they get prison haircuts; after which Ferdinand would let his hair grow again. In Act Two, Jan should have an eighties haircut, though Ferdinand could stay shaggy. Nigel should have seventies long hair in Act One and an eighties haircut in Act Two.

Rock 'n' Roll was first presented at the Royal Court Theatre, London, on 3 June 2006, and transferred to the Duke of York's Theatre on 22 July 2006, presented by Sonia Friedman Productions, Tulbart Productions, Michael Linnit for National Angels and Boyett Ostar Productions. The cast in order of appearance was as follows:

The Piper/Policeman 1/Stephen Edward Hogg
Esme (younger)/Alice Alice Eve
Jan Rufus Sewell
Max Brian Cox
Eleanor/Esme (older) Sinead Cusack
Gillian/Magda/Pupil Miranda Colchester
Interrogator/Nigel Anthony Calf
Ferdinand Peter Sullivan
Milan/Policeman 2/Jaroslav Martin Chamberlain
Lenka Nicole Ansari
Candida Louise Bangay

Director Trevor Nunn
Designer Robert Jones
Costume Designer Emma Ryott
Lighting Designer Howard Harrison
Sound Designer Ian Dickinson
Associate Director Paul Robinson
Company Voice Work Patsy Rodenburg

Characters

in order of appearance

The Piper
Esme (younger)
Jan
Max
Eleanor
Gillian
Interrogator
Ferdinand
Milan
Magda
Policeman 1
Policeman 2
Lenka
Nigel
Esme (older)
Alice
Stephen
Candida
Deirdre
Waiter

Esme in Act One and Alice are to be played by the same actress; similarly Eleanor and Esme in Act Two.

Further doubling (or tripling) is optional. The intention is that the twenty characters may be played by a company of twelve. The Royal Court used a company of eleven, with the result that Milan became Policeman 2 and also usurped the Waiter; however, this is not the preferred option.

ROCK 'N' ROLL

Act One

Blackout.

The Piper is heard.

Then, night in the garden. The Piper is squatting on his heels high up on the garden wall, his wild dark hair catching some light, as though giving off light. His pipe is a single reed like a penny whistle. He plays for Esme, who is sixteen, a flower child of the period: 1968.

Light from the interior catches Esme dimly, her flowing garment, her long golden hair.

The interior shows part of a dining room, lowly lit by a lamp. There is a walk-through frontier between the room and the 'unlit' garden, which is leafy with a stone-flagged part large enough for a garden table and two or three chairs.

The Piper pipes the tune and then sings.

The Piper
'Lean out of your window,
Golden Hair,
I heard you singing
In the midnight air.
My book is closed,
I read no more . . .'

Jan enters the interior from within, going to the garden, into the spill of light. He is twenty-nine. His Czech accent is not strong.

The Piper laughs quietly to himself and vanishes, a spring-heeled jump into dark.

Esme Who's that? Jan?

Jan (*a greeting*) *Ahoj*. What are you doing?

Esme Did you see him?

Jan Who?

Esme Pan!

Jan Pan. Where?

Esme There.

Jan No. Did he have goat's feet?

Esme I couldn't see. He played on his pipe and sang to me.

Jan Very nice. Have you got any left?

Esme Don't believe me, then.

Jan Who said I don't believe you?
    I came to say goodbye to Max.

Esme Where are you going?

Jan Prague.

Esme Why? Oh, yeah. What about the summer teach-in? Will you come back to Cambridge?

Jan (*shrugs: don't know*) I'm leaving everything here.

Esme Your records?

Jan No. Everything else. But now I must go home.

Esme What, to help the Russians?

Jan No.

Esme Max thinks it's great about the Russians.

Jan No, he doesn't. We don't.

Esme Ha – some Communists you are!

Overheard by Max, coming from indoors. He's nearly fifty-one, a bruiser.

Max Go to bed, you . . . flower child.

Esme I'd like to go to Prague, poke flowers into the ends of their gun barrels.

Jan I'm glad I saw you, Esme.

Esme Peace and love, Jan.
I want to give you something to take.

Jan What something?

Esme I don't know. Come and see before you go. Will you?

Jan Yes.

Esme In case you die. Peace and love, Pa.

Max Wouldn't that be nice? Keep your pop groups down, Mum's just managed to get off.

Esme (*mocks*) 'Pop groups . . .'

She goes into the house.

Max (*uncharmed*) Sweet sixteen.

Jan So. Some sunny day. Thank you.

Jan hesitates, starts to go. Max turns dangerous.

Max Sovereignty was never the point. You know that.

Jan (*cautious, calming*) Okay.

Max Being Czech, being Russian – German, Polish – fine, *vive la différence*, but going it alone is going against the alliance, you know this.

Jan Okay.

Max It's comfort and joy to capitalism, comfort and joy, and your bloody Dubcek did this, not the Soviets – I speak as one who's kicked in the guts by nine-tenths of anything you can tell me about Soviet Russia.

Jan Why have you stayed in the Party?

Max Because of the tenth, because they made the revolution and no one else.

Jan So okay.

Max Prague bloody Spring? It was never about the *workers*.

Jan (Okay.)

Max No, it's not okay, you little squit. I picked you out. I put my thumbprint on your forehead. I said, '*You*. I'll take *you*,' because you were serious and you knew your Marx . . . and at the first flutter of a Czech flag you cut and run like an old woman still in love with Masaryk.

Jan Dubcek is a Communist.

Max (*roused*) No – *I'm* a Communist, I'd be a Communist with Russian tanks parked in King's Parade, you mummy's boy.

Jan (*insists*) A reform Communist.

Max Like a nun who gives blow-jobs is a reform nun. I have to walk this off. Tell Esme to wait up for me, in case Eleanor wakes. Then fuck off back to Prague. I'm sorry about the tanks.

Blackout and 'I'll Be Your Baby Tonight' by Bob Dylan.

A smash cut into bright day in the same place, with Max there and Eleanor already speaking. She is in her late forties. She sits at a garden table. She has her work with her.

Eleanor He said you knew him, he was a friend of Jan.

Max *(catching up)* He was *Czech*.

Eleanor He said to tell you Jan wasn't coming back, he asked for his things . . .

Max Who asked?

Eleanor Milos. Milan. I was a bit thrown at the time because I opened the door to him without my falsy and didn't catch on till he kept staring at my face – he daren't drop his eyes, it scared him. Doesn't she know she's only got one tit? I should keep a bow and arrow handy to put people at their ease – yes, it's toxophily, the big T, irreversible, thank you, no sacrifice is too great.

Max silenced, to her name.

Max Eleanor.

Eleanor He was sucking on a lozenge, he offered me one, gazing into my eyes and breathing eucalyptus at me like a koala caught in the headlights.

Max perhaps touches her face.

Max He was probably staring for the same reason as me the first time I . . . It was never your, your breast, it was always your face. I love your face.

Eleanor You loved my tits, that's why breasts is plural.

Max It makes no difference, you know.

Eleanor Well, it does to me!

Max Yes – yes, of course it does, I only meant . . . you know, it makes no (difference).

He makes to hold her, Eleanor fights him off, tearfully angry.

Eleanor If it makes no difference, Max, you don't have to stop making love to me from behind, it's all right – all right?

Suddenly in freefall, they clutch, competing in apology and comfort.

Max (*finally*) My Amazon. Just don't lose half your bum, that's all.

She wipes her eyes, fails at a laugh, blows her nose.

Eleanor I had Amazons in my doctorate . . . false etymologies. *Mazos*, a breast; *amazos*, breastless. It makes sense if you're Greek, but the Amazons weren't Greek and didn't speak Greek, so I said the one-breast thing was a language glitch and quite late – nothing about being a tit short in Homer, only killer feminists all round, and vase painters did two-breasted Amazons – case proved, done and dusted. And now this. It makes you wonder. Anyway, I've got my Sapphist showing up . . .

Max (*protests*) You're on sick leave.

Eleanor So she's coming here. (*a quick kiss*) It's all right now.

Max Eleanor.
Um, why did he ask *you*, the eucalyptus-lozenge man?

Eleanor You weren't here.

Max Why would I be here?

Eleanor Oh, and someone from BBC Radio –

Max I'd be in College.

Eleanor The Czechs have agreed to a temporary occupation, and did you want to comment et cetera?

Max (*laughs*) I bet they have.

Eleanor Anyway, I said no, you didn't.

Max I wouldn't have minded.

Eleanor You would. Max Morrow putting the other side
. . . it'd be Christmas come early for every ex-Communist
who dreams about you.

Doorbell.

That's her.

Max Esme's there.

*Faint music – the Rolling Stones' 'High Tide and
Green Grass' album.*

The 'other side' needs putting. You can't teach the West
anything about occupation.

Eleanor That's a bit subtle for some – tanks is tanks and
it's on TV, so just do what you did last time when they
occupied Hungary.

Max What did I do?

Eleanor Ate shit and shut up.

Esme (*distant*) Mum!

Eleanor (*bawls*) I know!
I'm a frightened woman. That's all it is. I'm sorry.

Esme (*closer*) Mum . . .!

Eleanor (*calls*) All *right*!
It's my Sappho tutorial. Do you mind?

*Esme pops in and straight out, wearing a red-leather
bomber jacket.*

Esme (*voice down*) Lezzie lesson . . .

Eleanor (*calls after her*) In here!
Remind me to clout her. Do I look all right?

Max (*looks*) All present and correct.

Eleanor I mean my *face* –

Max (Oh . . .)

Eleanor – do I look as if I've been crying?

Max No. Sorry, I'm (sorry) –
(*letting go, angrily*) I'm down to one belief, that
between theory and practice there's a decent fit – not
perfect but decent: ideology and a sensible fair society, it's
my double helix and I won't be talked out of it or done
out of it or shamed out of it. We just have to be better.

*Gillian, a student who dresses 'sensibly', carrying
books etc., comes into the garden uncertainly. Max
ignores her, goes past her into the house. Eleanor
greets Gillian and smiles her into the second chair.*
   A door slams: Max leaving the house.
   *Esme's music becomes louder. Eleanor excuses
herself and goes into the house. Gillian puts on her
glasses and gets out her essay.*
   Esme's music cuts out.
   Eleanor and Esme are heard rowing briefly.
   Eleanor returns to her place.

Eleanor Right. Off you go.

Gillian It's Fragment 130.

Eleanor Eros the knee-trembler.

Gillian (*reads*) '*Eros deute m'o lusimeles donei
glukupikron amachanon orpeton . . .*' 'Eros, once more,
loosens my limbs, stirs me, bitter-sweet naughty boy –'

Eleanor (Naughty?)

Gillian '– he steals in.'

Eleanor And why not 'sweet-bitter'?

Gillian 'The interesting word here is Sappho's invention *glukupikron,* sweet-bitter, with no known . . .'

Eleanor Really, Gillian? It's a nice compound, but the *interesting* word here is *amachanon*. Naughty doesn't get near it. What's the root?

Gillian I . . . *Machan . . . ?*

Eleanor Right. *Machan.* Think 'machine' . . .

Gillian (*confused*) (Think-machine?)

Eleanor . . . contrivance, device, instrument, in a word, technology. So, *a-machanon – un-*machine, *non-*machine. Eros is *amachanon,* he's spirit as opposed to machinery, Sappho is making the distinction. He's not naughty, he's – what? Uncontrollable. Uncageable.

Gillian (*bursts out*) But I think I've found a precedent for *glukupikron*!

Eleanor (*pause*) Really? Try me.

Gillian (*gathers herself*) ' . . . Sappho's invention *glukupikron,* sweet-bitter, with no known precedent. *Or is there?* The lacuna in front of *pikros,* Fragment 88A, line 19, is suggestive –'

Eleanor Have you been to look?

Gillian Look?

Eleanor At the papyrus. It's in Oxford in the Ashmolean.

Gillian No.

Eleanor Well, I have. If that's a lacuna I'm a monkey's uncle –

But Gillian has broken – she gathers up her stuff in a rush, failing to keep back her tears, and leaves the way she came . . . passing Esme entering.

Esme (*reproaching Eleanor*) Mum . . .!

Eleanor There isn't *time* . . .!

Blackout and 'It's All Over Now' by the Rolling Stones.

A smash cut to:
Prague. Office interior. A table, two chairs, a coffee cup, a plate of biscuits.
Jan sits facing his Interrogator, a youngish middle-ranking bureaucrat.
The Interrogator has files to refer to.

Interrogator So, Doctor . . . Have a biscuit. They tell me your luggage consisted entirely – I mean *entirely* – of socially negative music.

Jan Yes, I'm thinking of writing an article on socially negative music.

Interrogator (*deadpan*) Really? When our allies answered our call for fraternal assistance to save socialism in this country, thousands of Czechs and Slovaks who happened to be in the West decided to stay there. You, on the other hand, whom we requested to remain in Cambridge for Professor Morrow's . . . 'summer –' what?

Jan 'Teach-in'.

Interrogator 'Summer titchin', you rushed back to Prague. Why did you come home?

Jan To save socialism.

Interrogator I'm afraid you're not taking us seriously. You have one doctorate from Charles University and nearly a doctorate from Cambridge University, so you're thinking two doctors must be cleverer than one official in the Ministry of the Interior. I take it you're Jewish.

Jan No, that's not what – What?

Interrogator (*referring to a file*) You left Czechoslovakia just before the Occupation.

Jan No, in April, for the summer term.

Interrogator The Occupation. The Nazis. Hitler.

Jan Oh! Yes. Yes. The Occupation. Sorry.

Interrogator Because you were Jewish.

Jan So it seemed.

Interrogator Well, are you or aren't you?

Jan Yes.

Interrogator Right. I don't know why you make such a thing about it. So, a babe in arms, you left with your parents and spent the war in England.

Jan Yes.

Interrogator And you came back here . . . with your mother in January 1948.

Jan Yes. My father was killed in the war. My mother is still alive, in Gottwaldov.

Interrogator Strange for you, coming back. A little English schoolboy.

Jan We always spoke Czech at home in England. And ate *spanelske ptacky*, *knedliky*, *buchty* . . .

Interrogator But you haven't had a biscuit! Help yourself.

Jan Thanks. Actually, I won't have one.

Interrogator You *won't* have one?

Jan I mean, I don't want one, thank you.

Interrogator Go on, have a biscuit, there's plenty.

Jan It's all right.

Interrogator So have one.

Jan takes a biscuit.
 The Interrogator watches him eat it, smiling encouragingly.

Good?

Jan Lovely.

Interrogator *Lovely?* It's only a biscuit. They're a bit stale, actually, don't you think?

Jan A bit.

Interrogator Lovely and stale, then, would you say?

Jan If you like.

Interrogator There you are. It's amazing. I can apparently make you do and say anything I want – yet when it comes to something simple, my failure . . . (*He lifts and lets fall the thin file.*) . . . is complete. It wasn't much to ask in exchange for the privilege we allowed you . . . to establish friendly relations with your professor . . .

Jan (I did that.)

Interrogator (*ignoring*) . . . and make a report on his connections . . .

Jan I understand why you're disappointed, but, you know, Cambridge is, well, it's Cambridge, nothing happens there.

Interrogator How can you say that?

He picks up the thickest file.

Look at this.

Jan Well . . . what is it?

Interrogator The file on you in Cambridge.

Jan The file on me?

Interrogator (*opening the file*) For example, there was a guest lecture by Professor Vitak from Bratislava, and afterwards a small group adjourned to Professor Morrow's house to continue the discussion.

Jan I put that in.

Interrogator But not what was said.

Jan It wasn't interesting.

Interrogator What is interesting is not for you to decide. Here's another one – a reception at the Cambridge Union Labour Club: evidently you thought it wasn't interesting that a young woman, a Czech student of philology, made negative remarks about our policemen. (*He opens the thin file.*) So what do I read in your report? 'Party for socialist students at Labour Club. Many toasts to fraternal solidarity.'

Jan Well – okay – yes – but there was an ethical problem. Well, I'd been sleeping with her . . . I couldn't possibly . . . she would have been called home before her finals.

Interrogator Unless she was following instructions.

Jan Lenka? You're kidding.

Interrogator Who knows? But you'd think that two or even one and a half doctors of philosophy would consider the possibility. (*closing the file*) You're not clever, you're simple. And if you're not simple you're complicated. We're supposed to know what's going on inside people. That's why it's the Ministry of the Interior. Are you simple or complicated? Have another biscuit.

15

Jan Excuse me, but –

He stops and takes a biscuit, holds it.

Thank you. Excuse me, but when will I get my records back?

Interrogator That's what we're here to talk about.

Blackout and 'All Over Now' by the Plastic People of the Universe.
Optional: projections of photos of the Plastic People.

Smash cut to:
Prague. April 1969. Jan's living room.
Jan is busying himself, putting beer on the table, looking through his record albums.
Jan's record player is playing 'Venus in Furs' by the Velvet Underground.
A lavatory flushes. Ferdinand, a young man, about the same age as Jan, enters.

Ferdinand That's better.

Jan How were the Beach Boys? Did they do 'God Only Knows'?

Ferdinand They did everything. What's that?

Jan Velvet Underground. 'Venus in Furs'. What do you think?

Ferdinand I don't get it.

Jan It's okay. I'll . . .

Jan takes off the record and puts it reverently into its sleeve, which has a picture of a banana. Ferdinand looks through the other sleeves.

Got given it by a girl in Cambridge last year. Andy Warhol did the banana.

Ferdinand (*enviously*) You bastard . . . 'Sergeant Pepper', Cream, the Kinks . . .

Jan You're welcome to come and make tapes any time.

Ferdinand (*for the beer*) Thanks.

Jan So, how were the Beach Boys?

Ferdinand I have to say they were great. They dress like the children of apparatchiks but when they play you can't argue with it. They dedicated 'Break Away' to Dubcek. He was in the audience.

Jan Dubcek was in the audience?!

Ferdinand Well, he's got nothing else to do now Husák's taken his job. The Beach Boys live at the Lucerna! It's a historic moment.

Jan I suppose so. (*Takes his beer.*) Cheers.

Ferdinand Cheers. The Beach Boys.

Jan The Mothers of Invention. Cheers.

Ferdinand The Stones.

Jan The Rolling Stones live at the Lucerna.

Ferdinand At Strahov!

Jan (*in pain*) Stop, stop. Should I put on a record?

Ferdinand Why not?

Jan So . . . why, erm . . . what are you up to, Ferdinand?

Ferdinand Right now? Actually, I'm collecting signatures.

Ferdinand produces a single page. Jan reads it. It's brief.

Jan Right.

Jan gives it back and resumes choosing a record.

Fugs or Doors?

Ferdinand What?

Jan Fugs or Doors?

Ferdinand I don't care.

Jan Right.

Ferdinand Dubcek was shunted aside still telling us the reforms are on track. He said it again last week. Are you listening?

Jan Yes.

Ferdinand And now they're stalling on the censorship thing just like they stalled on the trade (union thing) . . .

A blast of music obliterates Ferdinand. He jumps up and stops the record.

What are you doing?

Jan Listening to the Doors – what are *you* doing?

Ferdinand Well, forget the Doors for a minute. This concerns you. You're a journalist.

Jan I'm a university lecturer. I just write articles.

Ferdinand That means you're a journalist.

Jan Okay, I'm a journalist, but nobody's censoring me.

Ferdinand Not up front, and that'll be next.

Jan You're such a defeatist!

Ferdinand *I'm* a defeatist?

Jan You can't face life without a guarantee. So you convince yourself everything's going to end badly. But look – when the Russians invaded, you would have bet on mass arrests, the government in gaol, everything banned, reformers thrown out of their jobs, out of the universities, the whole Soviet thing, with accordion bands playing Beatles songs. I thought the same thing. I came back to save rock 'n' roll, and my mother actually. But none of it happened. My mum's okay, and there's new bands ripping off Hendrix and Jethro Tull on equipment held together with spit. I was in the Music F Club where they had this amateur rock competition. The Plastic People of the Universe played 'Venus in Furs' from Velvet Underground, and I knew everything was basically okay.

Ferdinand What the fuck are you (talking about) –?

Jan I'm trying to tell you. For once this country found the best in itself. We've been done over by big powerful nations for hundreds of years but this time we refused our destiny.

Ferdinand It's not destiny, you moron, it's the neighbours worrying about *their* slaves revolting if we get away with it.

Jan Yes, and we scared the shit out of them – they thought they'd started World War Three. Because instead of some Czech stooge ready to take over like in Hungary in '56, all there was was a handful of Stalinists in hiding from a reform movement that refused to roll over. Now they're looking for the exit, and we're still in charge of creating socialism with a human face.

Ferdinand Except for Dubcek, you mean.

Jan Dubcek's a nice guy, but basically Cliff Richard – he had to go. Husák'll keep the hardliners on the B side.

Ferdinand I'm a bit – I feel a bit (dazed) – Let me tell you about defeatism. Defeatism is turning disaster into a moral victory.

Jan (*getting angry*) Can't you function unless you're losing? Czechoslovakia is now showing the way – a Communist society with proper trade unions, legal system, no censorship – progressive rock . . .

Ferdinand They closed down your paper!

Jan And we protested, and now we're publishing again.

Ferdinand With conditions.

Jan (*dismissively*) That's only about not being rude to the Russians – Husák's a realist, keep them off our backs.

Ferdinand So you won't sign.

Jan No.

Jan restarts the Velvet Underground record on the track 'Waiting for the Man'. As Ferdinand walks out without a word . . .

(*Shouts.*) What you need to do, Ferdinand, is cheer up.

Blackout and 'Waiting for the Man' continuing through amps.

Smash cut to:
    Exterior. Evening. February 1971.
    A man dressed for February, fur-capped and mufflered into anonymity, carrying a plastic bag, stands waiting.
    Jan in cold-weather gear enters in haste.

Jan I am so sorry! It started late, and – anyway, here I am – how are you? You should have waited inside! Come in – come in – it's upstairs –

He talks through the light change into his flat, where they remove their outer clothes, caps, scarves, gloves, Jan helping the man, who is revealed to be Max.

Is it warm enough? I went to a lecture. On Andy Warhol. Well, to be frank, the lecture was illustrated, you might say, with rock 'n' roll. How was the . . .? What – anniversary thing?

Max Somebody giving a speech for the so-many-years of . . .

Jan Of what?

Max I forget. I didn't go. With these jamborees, if you want to know the score, it's best to skip the official programme.

Jan So now you know the score.

Max Yes.

He looks Jan over.

You look all right. But you're not teaching any more.

Jan No.

Max Serves you right.

Jan laughs.

How do you illustrate a lecture on Andy Warhol with rock 'n' roll?

Jan It's a little complicated. There's this band I like, the Plastic People of the Universe, last year they lost their professional licence – undesirable elements, you know . . .

Max Undesirable how?

Jan Their songs are morbid, they dress weird, they look like they're on drugs, and one time they sacrificed a chicken on stage, but otherwise it's a mystery. So now it's illegal for them to make a living from concert bookings. But Jirous, he's like their artistic director, he's legally an art historian, so he booked the Music F Club for a lecture on Andy Warhol, but – (*He plays air-guitar.*) – illustrated.

Max laughs.

Thank you for, you know, finding me.

Max (*holds up the bag*) I promised Esme.

Max gives the bag to Jan, then goes to his stuff and takes a bottle from his topcoat pocket.

Jan (*investigates the bag*) Oh . . . thank you!
And Eleanor . . . is she . . . ?

Max She's . . . doing fine. Glasses.

Jan Good!

Jan goes for two glasses.

Please tell her, from my heart, and to Esme also. How is Esme?

Max Nineteen and pregnant, and living in a commune.

Jan Oh. But a Communist!

Max Yes, we've done that one. She's trying to persuade Eleanor to live on wild garlic. Skol.

Jan Skol. Why?

Max The cancer came back.

Jan Fuck. I'm so . . .

Max Yes.

Jan Is she . . . ?

Max Still teaching. Throwing up and bald as a coot, but you know Eleanor . . .

Jan Yes. Bold as a . . . *coot?*

Max Not bold, bald. She's lost all her hair.

Jan Oh . . . yes.

Max And you. You've still got work at the paper?

Jan Technically yes, but now I work in the kitchens.

Max laughs.

Max Husák certainly made a fool of you.

Jan (*shrugs*) I was an optimist for . . . nine months. It was great. I had my own column.

Max A column about what?

Jan Anything I liked.

Max smiles at him broadly, mirthlessly.

It was a question of which way to be useful. It's not useful to be a critic of what is over and done. I was a critic of the future. It was my socialist right. But when I refused to sign the loyalty pledge I was purged into the kitchen. Kitchen porter! That was some purge, hey? Twelve hundred scientists. Eight hundred university professors!

Max Nine hundred.

Jan Ah – the score. Also half my fellow journalists. Self-censorship about the Russian occupation didn't save us. Loyalty meant kissing their Soviet arses. I would have tried to emigrate but . . .

Jan looks at the album – 'The Madcap Laughs' by Syd Barrett.

Huh . . .

Max What?

Jan (*misunderstanding*) She wrote on the sleeve. 'Now do you believe me?'

Max But what?

Jan (*absent*) Is it okay?

Max is seething. Jan doesn't notice. He moves to put the record on.

Max You would have emigrated but what?

Jan Yes . . . I was offered a job in Frankfurt . . . but I don't know . . . German rock bands . . .

Syd Barrett (*sings, on record*)
'Lean out of your window,
Golden Hair,
I heard you singing
In the midnight air.' (*Continues.*)

Max (*erupts*) I never heard anything so pathetic. Do everybody a favour, go and live in the West, it's where you belong. You bedwetter! If it wasn't for eleven million Soviet military dead, your little country'd be a German province now – and you wouldn't be bellyaching about your socialist right to piss everywhere except in the toilet, you'd be smoke up the chimney.

Jan is shocked. He stops the record. Max refills his glass and drinks. He steadies himself.

I'm exactly as old as the October Revolution. I grew up with the fight against Fascism. In the slums, in Spain, the Arctic convoys . . . and today on a urinal wall I saw where someone had scrawled a hammer and sickle and a swastika joined by an equals sign. If I'd caught who did that, I'd probably have killed him. (*He drinks.*) And Esme thinks a Fascist is a mounted policeman at a demo in Grosvenor Square.

Jan So.

Max (*turns to him*) There's something which keeps happening to me. More and more now that I'm getting to be half-famous for not leaving the Communist Party. I meet somebody, it could be a visiting professor, or someone fixing my car, anyone . . . and what they all want to know, though they don't know how to ask, because they don't want to be rude, is – how come, when it's obvious even to them, *how come I don't get it?* And it's the same here. I meet some apparatchik working the system, and he's fascinated by me. He's never met a Communist before. I'm like the last white rhino. *Why don't I get it?*

Jan So why don't you?

Max Don't push it. A workers' state fits the case. What else but *work* lifts us out of the slime? Work does all the work. What the hell else?

Jan How about . . . ballet?

Max grins amiably, he's calm now.

Max 'From each according to his abilities, to each according to his needs'. What could be more simple, more rational, more beautiful? It was the right idea in the wrong conditions for fifty years and counting. A blip. Christ, we waited long enough for someone to have it.

Jan A blip. Stalin killed more Russians than Hitler. Perhaps we aren't good enough for this beautiful idea. This is the best we can do with it. Marx knew we couldn't be trusted. First the dictatorship, till we learned to be good, then the utopia where a man can be a baker in the morning, a lawmaker in the afternoon and a poet in the evening. But we never learned to be good, so look at us. A one-legged man showed up at my school once.

He waited outside the classroom. It turned out the man with one leg had come to say goodbye to our teacher. Afterwards, the teacher explained to us his friend lost his leg in the war, so as a special favour he'd been given permission to go and live near his sister somewhere in north Bohemia. 'You see,' our teacher said, 'how Communism looks after its war heroes.' So I put my hand up. God, I must have been stupid. I really thought it would be interesting for them, so I said in England anyone could live anywhere they liked, even if they had two legs. My mother was questioned and she lost her job at the shoe factory, but the point is the other kids in the class. They thought I was telling travellers' tales. They couldn't grasp the idea of a country where someone, anyone, could decide to move to another town and just go there. Suppose everybody wanted to live in Bohemia when their job is in Moravia! How would such a society *work*?

Max And you didn't explain?

Jan Explain what?

Max How English society works. How everyone's free to have lunch at the Ritz and it's absolutely legal to be unemployed.

Jan Your problems are yours, you fix them, okay? I love England. I would like to live for ever in my last English schoolboy summer. It was exceptional, you know? 1947, endless summer days, I collected birds' eggs, and the evenings so long you couldn't sleep for the light, listening to the farmer's boy calling the cattle home. And the winter was amazing that year. A Christmas card winter. My mother knew all the songs. She baked *svestkove buchty* for my friends, and sang 'We'll Meet Again' in a terrible accent over the washtub. I was happy.

Max Jesus Christ.

Jan If I was English I wouldn't care if Communism in Czechoslovakia reformed itself into a pile of pig shit. To be English would be my luck. I would be moderately enthusiastic and moderately philistine, and a good sport. I would be kind to foreigners in a moderately superior way, and also to animals except for the ones I kill, and I would live a decent life, like most English people. How many voted for the Communist Party, Max?

Max About two-tenths of one per cent. It's called the parliamentary route to socialism.

Jan You got the strange gods vote: Marxism, Fascism, anarchism kept on the side of the plate like a little bit of salt to bring out the flavour of English moderation. A thousand years of knowing who you are gives a people confidence in its judgement. Words mean what they have always meant. With us, words change meaning to make the theory fit the practice. We eat salt. Come on in, Max! Give me your place!

Max My *place*? My *place* can't be filled by a snivelling idealist. You don't get it either. Parliamentary democracy is a theory, too. The meaning changes to fit the practice.

Jan (*laughs*) Oh, you're good, Max, but when were you ever arrested for saying it? Or anything? Independent courts is not theoretical! You can call the government fools and criminals but the law is for free speech, the same for the highest and the lowest, they can't touch you, the law is constant – and yet, what you have set your heart on, Max, the only thing that will make you happy, is that the workers own the means of production. I would give it to you gladly if I could keep the rest.

Max turns ugly.

Max What do you want it for?

Jan To live free.

Max The little diddums! – Still sucking on philosophy's tit! For you, freedom means, 'Leave me alone.' For the masses it means, 'Give me a chance.' Social relations are economic, as I thought we'd agreed at Cambridge. You, me and Marx . . .

Jan So. Some sunny day.

Max So, at Cambridge, why were you pretending to be what you were not?

Max leaves.
    After a moment, Jan puts the needle on the record.

Syd Barrett (*sings, on record*)
    'Lean out of your window,
    Golden Hair,
    I heard you singing
    In the midnight air . . .'

The sound fades out. Jan continues to listen.

Exterior – continuous.
    Milan on a street bench – who may have been visible waiting and watching throughout the scene – stands up to meet Max approaching.

Milan Max . . . *Ahoj.* (*Reproachfully.*) I left you a message at the hotel.

Max Milan . . . that thing in Cambridge in '68 . . . it was a one-off, a titbit, an accident. A goodwill gesture. There's no more where that came from. I'm not worth cultivating.

Milan (*cheerfully*) You're too modest. How is your old pupil?

Milan takes out a small tin of lozenges and puts one delicately into his mouth.

Max Jan? He learned nothing.

Max and Milan leave.
Jan is still listening to the record.

Syd Barrett (*sings, on record*)
'. . . singing and singing a merry air,
Lean out of your window,
Golden Hair . . .'

Blackout – 'Astronomy Domine' by Pink Floyd
picking up thirty seconds in.

Smash cut to morning and silence. Summer 1972. Jan is
looking at a sheet of paper. The lavatory flushes, heard
through its open door.

Jan (*raising his voice*) I'm supposed to sign this?

A young woman enters in her slip: Magda.

Magda Aren't you going to work?

Jan Magda, when did Ferdinand leave this?

Magda He was at Klamovka. We waited for you.

She smells him carefully like a dog, half-serious.

Where were you, then?

Jan At the police station. As a witness. Jirous got shoved
around by a drunk outside the party, and two cops
sprayed his eyes and arrested him. They let him go this
morning.

Magda That's good, now they've got your name down as
a witness for a dissident.

Jan He's not a dissident, he's a hooligan. The band was
great, anyway . . . a lot of new material.

Magda You should get a tambourine and go full-time like Linda with Paul.

Jan I can't afford to turn amateur. Haven't you got lectures?

Jan looks at the piece of paper again.

Magda I can't face it this morning. It's you who's late, Jan.

Jan They changed my shift. Did Ferdinand ask you to sign his petition?

Magda Of course not. Some of us have careers to study for.

She goes out to continue dressing.

Jan (*laughs at the paper*) It's so polite. It doesn't protest against the sentences, it's just please dear kind Dr Husák, please be generous and include these three intellectuals in the amnesty next Christmas out of the goodness of your heart so they can go back to their families . . .

Magda comes back in a skirt, doing up her blouse.

Magda So will you sign it?

Jan No, I won't sign it. First because it won't help Hubl and the others, but mainly because helping them is not its real purpose. Its real purpose is to let Ferdinand and his friends feel they're not absolutely pointless. It's just moral exhibitionism.

Magda What's moral exhibitionism?

Jan All they're doing is exploiting the prisoners' misfortune to draw attention to themselves. If they're so concerned for the families they should go and do something useful for the families, instead of – for all they know – making things worse for the prisoners.

Magda Well, you'll be able to tell him that.

She looks for and finds her shoes.

Jan Thought you said you couldn't face it. Hey, Magda, who's been at my records?

Magda Ferda borrowed one.

Jan When?

Magda Maybe two. I think one with the cows.

Jan 'Atom Heart Mother'!

Magda He wanted to make tapes.

Jan (*looking for a record*) He's taken 'Madcap Laughs'.

Magda What?

Jan My Syd Barrett!

Magda He said he'd bring them back before you even noticed.

Jan When the hell would that be?!

There's a scratching at the door. Jan jumps up and opens the door – to Ferdinand, who has the missing records in a bag.

There's a bell, you bastard.

Ferdinand *Ahoj.*

Magda They changed his shift.

She kisses Jan and leaves.
Jan takes the bag, takes the records out of their sleeves, looks at them, puts them back. He relaxes a bit.

Ferdinand (*meanwhile*) Jan, Jan . . . Hey, how about that? Pink Floyd without Syd Barrett, and Syd Barrett without Pink Floyd.
How long have you had these?

Jan A while.

Ferdinand What happened?

Jan The Floyd dumped Barrett.

Ferdinand It shows.

Jan He was out of it with drugs.

Ferdinand He *sounds* out of it. But I love him.

Ferdinand finds his petition.
  Jan looks at the sleeve of the 'Madcap Laughs'
album and removes the disc.

Jan He went home to his mum in Cambridge. He comes
from Cambridge. I nearly saw him once, or maybe not.
A girl I know thinks she saw him and he sang to her . . .
only, she didn't know it was him. But she was high a lot
of the time, so I don't know . . . maybe it was the great
god Pan.

Jan puts the record on the player.

Ferdinand Will you sign this?

Jan No.

Syd Barrett (*sings, on record*)
  'I really love you and I mean you,
  The star above you crystal blue,
  Well oh baby my hair's on end about you . . .'

Blackout and 'Jugband Blues' by Pink Floyd.

Smash cut to night and silence.
  Spring 1974.
  *Ferdinand is reading a piece of paper. Jan is watching
him nervously.*

Jan Underground concerts are so rare now, kids from all over the country got the word and found their way to this nowhere place. So did busloads of police, with dogs. They stopped the concert and herded everyone to the railway station and through a tunnel under the tracks, and in the tunnel the police laid into everybody with truncheons. Rock 'n' roll!

Ferdinand So, what am I supposed to do with this?

Jan Get your friends to sign it.

Ferdinand What friends?

Jan You know, those banned writers and intellectuals you hang out with.

Ferdinand And this would be different from moral exhibitionism, would it?

Jan Yeah. A genuine moral action.

Ferdinand Oh, good. How is that, by the way?

Jan Well, because you've got no interest in these kids and they've got no interest in you.

Ferdinand That's the difference?

Jan Yeah, they don't care about politics . . . If people want to pick a fight with the government, that's their business.

Ferdinand They should take what comes, you mean.

Jan No . . . well, yeah . . . Perhaps you're missing the point.

Ferdinand Perhaps you'd like a smack in the mouth, but the difference is still eluding me.

Jan (*roused*) These are schoolkids, they'll get expelled and end up with the lowest work available in the

33

paradise of full employment, and what I'm saying is they didn't pick the fight. They didn't ask for anything except to be left alone for a while. It's not just the music, it's the oxygen. You know what I mean.

Ferdinand Why don't you get your friend Jirous to sign it?

Jan He's in gaol.

Ferdinand What for?

Jan Free expression. Somebody in a pub called him a big girl, so Jirous called him a bald-headed Bolshevik, and he turned out to be state security.

Ferdinand Yes, well, with Jirous you never know. Maybe insulting people in pubs is his idea of art.

Jan He thinks you're a bunch of tossers, too.

Ferdinand Does he?

Jan The 'official opposition'.
    The fans just want to be left alone to do their thing.

Ferdinand This isn't about the fans, it's about the band.

Jan Same thing.

Ferdinand (*getting angry*) You want me to ask serious men –

Jan Women, too, would be good.

Ferdinand – who are working in boiler rooms and timberyards –

Jan And breweries, right – famous odd job men.

Ferdinand – to invite the police to arrest them –

Jan Arrest them for what?

Ferdinand – so that your druggy drop-out weirdo friends with hair down to here can be allowed to do their own thing? You're an arsehole!

Jan That's a no, then.

Jan takes the petition back.

Ferdinand You're a political imbecile. There's no leverage in asking people to come out for people people don't give a shit about.

Jan Relax, Ferdinand.

Ferdinand I mean, who are they?

Jan Forget it. How's Magda?

Ferdinand What?

Jan How's –

Ferdinand She's fine – in fact, I forgot – she sends her love . . .

Jan Her love?

Ferdinand Let me explain –

Jan No, I get it.

Ferdinand You don't get it.

Jan Send her mine.

Ferdinand What?

Jan Should I put on a record?

Ferdinand No, let me explain. I don't believe in cultural hierarchy. Dvorak did his thing, the Plastic People do their thing . . . I do my thing – fine, the more the merrier and everyone's welcome. Except that none of us is welcome as things are. Except for Dvorak. But – my point is –

Jan I don't really want to –

Ferdinand Who's going to change things for the rest? Not the ones who just want to be left alone. The Plastics

35

won't change things so Vaculík and Grusa can publish their books. But *we're* putting ourselves on the line for a society where the Plastics can play their music.

Jan Excellent point.

Ferdinand Fuck you, just answer me one question. You've read Havel's letter to Husák?

Jan No.

Ferdinand That wasn't the question. But Havel has written this open letter about what's gone wrong in Czechoslovakia, the apathy, the spiritual paralysis, the self-destructive tendency of what he calls post-totalitarian –

Jan Jesus, Ferdinand! What's the question?

Ferdinand Who's got the best chance of getting Husák's attention – Havel or the Plastic People of the Universe?

Jan The Plastics.

Ferdinand I'll put it another way. Who's going to lay bare the ideological contradictions of bureaucratic dictatorship? Us intellectuals, or –?

Jan The Plastics. Why do you think you're walking around and Jirous is in gaol?

Ferdinand Because he insulted a secret policeman.

Jan No, because the policeman insulted *him*. About his hair. Jirous doesn't cut his hair. It makes the policeman angry, so he starts something and it ends with Jirous in gaol. But what is the policeman angry about? What difference does long hair make? The policeman is angry about his fear. The policeman's fear is what makes him angry. He's frightened by indifference. Jirous doesn't *care*. He doesn't care enough even to cut his hair. The policeman isn't frightened by *dissidents*! Why should he be? Policemen *love* dissidents, like the Inquisition loved heretics. Heretics give meaning to the defenders of the faith. Nobody cares more than a heretic. Your friend Havel cares so much he writes a long letter to Husák. It makes no odds whether it's a love letter or a protest letter. It means they're playing on the same board. So Husák can relax, he's made the rules, it's his game. The population plays the other way, by agreeing to be bribed by places at university, or an easy ride at work . . . they care enough to keep their thoughts to themselves, their haircuts give nothing away. But the Plastics don't care at all. They're unbribable. They're coming from somewhere else, from where the Muses come from. They're not heretics. They're pagans.

Blackout and 'It's Only Rock 'n' Roll' by the Rolling Stones.

Smash cut to daylight and silence.
Autumn 1975.
Jan and Ferdinand sit almost in suspended animation. Ferdinand's hair has been cut short. The lavatory flushes.
A man comes out of the bathroom, doing up his flies. He has a leather jacket, the jacket of choice for secret policemen.

Policeman 1 (*smirks*) Apologies. My aim was off.

.A second Policeman stands at Jan's record collection.

Okay?

Policeman 2 Okay.

The Policemen leave together.
Ferdinand is phlegmatic. Jan leaps up.

Jan Oosh, whooof, shweez, hey, jesus, jeezuss . . .

Jan goes to look in the bathroom, and returns grimacing.

(*scared*) What did they want?

Ferdinand They didn't want anything.

Jan Then why did they come up?

Ferdinand They were bored, probably. Usually they hang about outside.

Jan Outside my place?

Ferdinand Outside anywhere I go. (*Pause.*) I won't come here, if you like.

Jan The thing is, I don't feel grown-up enough for prison. That's one thing. I'm definitely afraid of prison.

Ferdinand That's nothing to be ashamed of.

Jan (*snappish*) I'm not ashamed of it.

He becomes accusing.

It's normal to be afraid of prison. Normal people don't do things that might send them to prison. I can't even remember what you did, or who it was supposed to help. Of course, I understand it was for being heroic, I just forget the details. You must be bloody stupid going to prison for something I've forgotten before you come out, frankly. Heroism isn't honest work, the kind that keeps the world going round. It offends normal people and frightens them. It seems to be about some private argument the heroes are having with the government on our behalf, and we never asked you.

Ferdinand Relax, Jan.

Jan Well, it's very annoying. Heroic acts don't spring from your beliefs. I believe the same as you do. They spring from your character. It's not the action of a friend to point out that your character is more heroic than mine. It pisses me off. Why do you do it? You'll be insufferable now.

Ferdinand Do you complain to Jirous?

Jan No. Jirous's character is heroic and there's nothing to be done about it. He was a heroic baby.

Ferdinand I met him in prison.

Jan Did you? How did he look with a haircut?

Ferdinand He explained about the hair. The tempter says, 'Cut your hair just a little, and we'll let you play.' Then the tempter says, 'Just change the name of the band and you can play.' And after that, 'Just leave out this one song' . . . It is better not to start by cutting your hair, Jirous said – no, it is *necessary*. Then nothing you do can possibly give support to the idea that everything is in order in this country. Why couldn't you have explained this? I would have signed your hopeless letter. Other bands have better musicians but the Plastics are the only band safe from the desire for recognition. In the alternative culture, success is failure. Look what happens in the West, Jirous says.

Jan has calmed down. He selects a record to play.

Jan Yeah . . . the Grateful Dead must be so envious of the Plastics . . .

The record starts to play – 'Chinatown Shuffle' by the Grateful Dead.

(*after a moment*) How's Magda?

Ferdinand What?

Jan How's Magda?

Ferdinand I don't know.

Jan nods sympathetically. They sit listening.
    Blackout and the Grateful Dead continue through amps.

Smash cut to Cambridge. May 1976. Interior and garden.
    The dining table is cleared for a tutorial.
    Lenka, aged twenty-nine, is waiting for Eleanor. Lenka personifies a period look from her granny glasses to her smock and sandals. She carries her books in a canvas shoulder-bag. Her hair is long and unkempt. Lenka has a Czech accent.
    Max is sitting in the garden with Nigel, who is aged about thirty.
    Eleanor enters the dining area, wearing a tea cosy for a hat.

Eleanor (*entering*) Right. Sorry. Off we go.

    They need a few seconds to get launched.

Nigel Are you still a member of the Communist Party, Max?

Max Yes.

Nigel I find that fascinating.

Max I know. (*Shouts for help.*) Nell! Nigel's here!

    Eleanor makes an impatient sound, gets up, goes
    swiftly to the frontier between indoors and outdoors.

Eleanor Shush – it's Alice's nap.

    Indoors, a five-year-old starts calling for 'Granny'.

Oh, for heaven's sake!

Nigel Should I –?

Eleanor No. Hello, Nigel.

Eleanor hurries back through the dining area.

(*to Lenka*) Sorry.

Eleanor leaves towards the child, already addressing endearments.

Nigel Was that a tea cosy on her head?

Max Yes.

Nigel (*pause*) Do you mind if I ask you a question?

Max She didn't like me saying you couldn't tell her wig was a wig.

Nigel No, not about that. But with Communism, my paper wouldn't be allowed to criticise the government, or even . . . well, you know what I mean. If you had your way, the *Cambridge Evening News* would be a very different sort of newspaper. As would all the media. Well, you're much cleverer than me. Obviously. So my question is: am I missing something?

Max Yes.

Max gets up and goes indoors.

Lenka Hello.

Max Hello. I'm Max.

Lenka I know. We met once with Jan.

Max Jan's friend.

Lenka Lenka.

Max Lenka. He went home.

Lenka I stayed.

Max Of course. Philology?

Lenka And Classical Studies.

Nigel comes passing through.

Nigel I'll go and rescue her.

He leaves.

Lenka Eleanor is wonderful!

Max So, what . . .?

Lenka Consciousness in Sappho.

Max Oh, well, yes, Eleanor's your man for Sappho.

Lenka But you for consciousness.

Lenka smiles at him.
Eleanor comes back, now wearing a wig.

Eleanor Sorry. I hope I didn't frighten you. (*to Max*) You might have told me. What are you doing home anyway?

A passing kiss.

Max Don't see enough of Esme.

Eleanor Well, as you see, Lenka –

Max Can I listen in?

Eleanor What? No!

Max Fly on the wall.

Eleanor In the ointment, more like.

Lenka I don't mind, Eleanor.

Eleanor I do.

Max Oh, come on, consciousness is my sack, after all.

Eleanor I think you mean your bag, but be that as it (may) –

Lenka Actually, I read your book, Professor Morrow.

Max *Class and Consciousness* or *Masses and Materialism*?

Eleanor Sappho's not in there, is she?

Max Ha-ha, Cecil B. De Morrow; no, she isn't.

Lenka It made things clear for me.

Max I'm definitely staying.

Lenka I think you're wrong, you see.

Max Great.

He sits down opposite Eleanor, rubbing his palms together. Lenka's place is diagonal to Max down the table.

Eleanor Max.

Max Esme's going to be here in a minute to pick up Nigel and the kid. (*to Lenka*) Child-minding. She's a doting granny, don't pass it around.

Eleanor laughs, pleased. Max squeezes her hand. A moment.

(*to Lenka*) Go ahead.

Eleanor You don't know the text.

Max Fine. Call me Max.

Eleanor She doesn't have to call you anything, because you're not –

Max Fine.

Eleanor gives Lenka the nod.

Eleanor Will you start?

Lenka (*pause*) No, you start. No, I'll start. (*Pause.*) My mind's gone blank.

Max All right, I'll start –

Eleanor (*shouts*) You don't even know –

Max Fine.

Eleanor I'll start. Sappho begins, 'He seems to me equal to a god . . .'

Lenka Right! – She begins not with the love object but with the man who's getting all the love object's attention – which to Sappho makes him seem equal to a god. I see it as a group of friends round a table having lunch maybe, and in the poem Sappho is describing what it's like to experience love and desire and jealousy. Because there, down the table, this *man* is leaning in to listen to her girl's sweet speaking and lovely laughing, and it's Sappho's *body* that goes beserk. Her *heart* jumps around like a bird beating its wings, her *eyes* stop seeing, her *tongue* breaks, her *ears* fill up with noise, her *skin* goes hot, then cold and clammy, her *body*'s out of control – it's all happening like that, in the third person, these *things* are behaving like that. Out there.

Eleanor But the first-person singular comes back – 'I'm green, I'm gone, dead or almost.'

Lenka So, okay. But the subjective experience of the objective world *when that world includes the poet* is obviously paradoxical –

Eleanor 'Obviously' is a word I don't allow. It usually means that something is far from obvious. For instance, can you lump together what's in Sappho's consciousness with what's physically 'out there' in the objective world, like the birds and the bees?

Max nods and does a thumbs-up: yes, you can.

44

Experiencing love is different from experiencing a bee sting.

Max converts the gesture into waggling his hand palm-down.

Lenka The paradox I mean is that Sappho is describing her own consciousness from outside itself, she describes the feeling of love as objectively as she might describe being stung by a bee.

Eleanor What she is *describing* is the physiology.

Max Same thing.

Eleanor (*smoothly*) Which is obviously not the same thing.

Max picks up on 'obviously'. Eleanor affects not to notice.

Seemingly not the same thing. When you say, 'I love you,' you're not saying 'Darling, I notice some rather unusual events in my body.'

Max nods vigorously to disagree.

Unless you're odd.

Max smiles at her.

Lenka (*agreeing*) Unless you have a materialist agenda.

Max smiles at Lenka.

Eleanor And anyway, Sappho's list of symptoms could be describing other causes, like fear or embarrassment, or influenza, for that matter.

Lenka Exactly! How do we know it's love? Because the poet knows! The mental separates from the physical. Sappho has a mental cognition of *love*; not influenza.

Max mimes despair.

45

If she's stung by a bee, she feels the sting, and she locates the bee in the objective world. If she's stung by love, she locates Aphrodite as the stinger.

Max is dumbfounded.

Eleanor Aphrodite?

Lenka Aphrodite exists for her. Like Eros. Like all the gods. They become the acting agent, and Sappho becomes the object acted upon.

Max Hang on.

Eleanor Yes, hang on. (*to Max*) You just be quiet.

Lenka 'Aphrodite, come to me!' she cries. And, 'Eros shook my mind like the wind shakes the oak trees' . . . 'Eros! – who melts my limbs, sweet-bitter rascal . . .'

Max puts his head on the table.

Eleanor There are some among us who possibly consider Aphrodite and Eros to be a sort of metaphor . . .

Lenka rounds on Max.

Lenka There are some among us who think knowledge is advanced when we give something a new name. Goodbye, Eros; hello, libido. Goodbye, Muses; hello, inspiration.

Max There are some among us who thought we'd liberated reason from our ancestral bog of myth and claptrap. Inspiration doesn't exist either, by the way, except as so many neuron-firings whizzing about the cortex.

Lenka Maybe we lost something older than reason, and stranger than your pinball machine which thinks it's in love.

Max Pinball machine isn't bad. It does love. It does inspiration. It does memory. It does *thought*. If mental is

separate from physical, how does it make Sappho go hot
and cold and deaf and blind at lunch?

Lenka I don't know. Sappho didn't know why things fall
to the floor. So what? They fell anyway. She looks down
the table and she is in love separate from her body. (*She
plays her trump.*) If it's an illusion, who's having it?

Max Not 'who' – 'what'. Her brain's having it.

Lenka Her mind?

Max Her mind *is* her brain. The brain is a biological
machine for thinking. If it wasn't for the merely technical
problem of understanding how it works, we could make
one out of – beer cans. It would be the size of a stadium
but it would sit there, going, 'I think, therefore I am.' (*to
Eleanor*) You're very quiet.

Eleanor Well, I've heard it before.

Lenka laughs and brings out her roll-your-own kit.

Lenka What you like about brains, Max, is that they all
work in the same way. What you don't like about minds
is that they don't. To you consciousness is subversive –
because *your* thing is the collective mind. But politics is
over. You're looking for revolution in the wrong place.
Consciousness is where it's at now. We have to rediscover
our human mystery in the age of technology. Have you
read *Zen and the Art of Motorcycle Maintenance*?

She slides a book down the table.

Borrow it.

Eleanor Is that grass, Lenka?

Lenka Yes, do you want some?

The child is heard from within. A car is heard tooting.

Eleanor No, thank you. And that's Esme. Sorry about
the interruptions.

Lenka Oh, no, it was good.

Eleanor I meant Alice.

Max (*put out*) I've never let anyone have the last word *yet*.

Lenka (*laughs*) I'm always available.

Eleanor Next time we might do a little Greek.

> *Eleanor goes out.*
> *Noises off and voices, Eleanor answering Alice.*
> *Lenka packs her shoulder-bag.*

Lenka That was really, you know, great . . .

Max (*declining her spliff*) Ah, no thanks.

Lenka I'm at Newnham.

Max Maybe I'll see Jan in the summer vac. I've been invited to Prague for a brain-science bunfight.

Lenka He's in prison, didn't you know?

Max No! No, I didn't.

Lenka Yeah. I heard he was one of the ones arrested.

Max One of what ones?

Lenka With the Plastic People of the Universe and –

Max The what? What, you mean the thing I was just – I was asked to sign a letter, along with a select bunch of the usual chest-beaters about some pop group – I had no idea Jan . . .

Lenka Did you sign it?

> *Eleanor comes back.*

Eleanor It's Esme, whom you don't see enough of – she's not coming in, she has to catch the shops.

48

Max Jan has been arrested.

Max goes out.

Lenka Yes. That's bad. (*Pause.*) Well, thanks. I'll see you when I've . . .

Eleanor (*pleasantly*) Good. And, Lenka, don't try to shag my husband till I'm dead, or I'll stick the art of motorcycle maintenance up your rancid cunt, there's a dear.

Eleanor drops the book into Lenka's shoulder-bag. Lenka gives a gasp, a sob, tries to speak, and leaves by the garden.
In the house there are sounds of departure, the door closing.
Eleanor remains still, in an exhaustion which she dissembles when Max returns, but she remains taut.

Max I say, I upset Esme . . . I told her about Jan, and she . . .

Eleanor Tsk, damn . . .

Max . . . sort of burst into tears. Did I miss something?

Eleanor Yes.

Max Do you think so? What, because she made me bring him pop music?

Eleanor She asked Jan to take her virginity.

Max What? When?

Eleanor His last night in England.

Max Oh. I'm glad I didn't sign that letter now.

Eleanor Jan told her not to be silly. He took one of her records instead.

Max Ah. How bourgeois of him. Well, all right. And now he's in the jug for some pop group thing, Lenka

49

says. I was asked to sign a protest. Had to suck my pen a bit. Should pop singers be locked up or given lots of money and treated like gods? That's a hard one. Listen, don't laugh but I think Lenka fancies me.

Eleanor Never.

Do you think there's anything, anything *at all* in what she's saying?

Max No. Consciousness is not where it's at. It doesn't determine the social order. It's the other way round.

Eleanor I don't mean about the social order.

Max To be human is to be joined together. Society! When the revolution was young and I was young, we were all made from a single piece of timber. The struggle was for socialism through organised labour, and that was that. What remains of those bright days of certainty? Where do I belong? The Party is losing confidence in its creed. If capitalism can be destroyed by anti-racism, feminism, gay rights, ecological good practice and every special interest already covered by the Social Democrats, is there a lot of point in being a Communist? – to spend one's life explaining: no, Stalin wasn't it, either? Why do people go on as if there's a danger we might forget Communism's crimes, when the danger is we'll forget its achievements? I've stayed in because they meant so much to me. Now that they seem to mean so little to anyone else, I sometimes think . . . Nell, what do you think? Do you think I . . . ?

Eleanor (*breaks*) I don't care! I don't care about it! Stay in – get out – I don't care, Max!

Max What is it? What's happened?

Eleanor It's you. My body is telling me I'm nothing without it, and you're telling me the same.

Max No . . . *No.*

Eleanor You are, Max! It's as if you're in cahoots, you and my cancer.

Max Oh, God – Nell.

He tries to hold her. Weeping, she won't be held.

Eleanor They've cut, cauterised and zapped away my breasts, my ovaries, my womb, half my bowel, and a nutmeg out of my brain, and I am undiminished, I'm exactly who I've always been. *I am not my body.* My body is nothing without *me*, that's the truth of it.

She tears open her dress.

Look at it, what's left of it. It does classics. It does half-arsed feminism, it does love, desire, jealousy and fear – Christ, does it do fear! – so who's the me who's still in one piece?

Max I know that – I know your mind is everything.

Eleanor (*furious*) Don't you dare, Max – don't you dare reclaim that word *now*. I don't want your 'mind' which you can make out of beer cans. Don't bring it to my funeral. I want your grieving soul or nothing. I do not want your amazing biological machine – I want what you love me with.

She hits bottom and stays there. Max waits, not comforting her. Then he crouches close to her.

Max But that's what I love you with. That's it. There's nothing else.

Her drowned face comes up.

Eleanor Oh, Max. Oh, Max. Now that did take some guts.

Max gathers her in and rocks her.
   Blackout and 'Welcome to the Machine' by Pink Floyd, three minutes and fifty seconds in.

Smash cut to:
November 1976. Jan's room.
Summer 1977. Prague exterior.

Jan's records have been smashed and scattered among torn-up album covers.
Jan enters, wearing cold-weather clothes. He stands looking at the debris.
He takes his top clothes off. He picks up a broken record and looks at the label.
Ferdinand, walks in, wearing cold-weather clothes. He has a plastic bag with an album in it. He stands stunned among the vinyl shards.

Ferdinand Shit.

Jan nods.

Bastards.

Jan nods.

Shit.

Jan nods.

Sorry.

Jan goes abruptly into the bathroom. Ferdinand waits.

Milan enters the exterior, in summer clothes and dark glasses. He sprawls on a bench.

The lavatory flushes. Jan comes in, wiping his mouth on the back of his wrists.
Ferdinand holds up the plastic bag, embarrassed.

I borrowed it when you were inside.

Jan grunts a laugh.

And then what with everything . . .

Jan Yeah. Amazing time. There wasn't one policeman at Jirous's wedding. The concert was a joy. I thought – okay, so eight years of the Plastics living underwater did the trick. Then they arrested *everybody*.

He looks at the record in the bag.

Beach Boys . . . You're so sweet, Ferdinand –

Ferdinand I knew you wouldn't mind.

Jan I owe you. That was a good letter, that first one.

Ferdinand I didn't write it.

Jan Well, I didn't think you'd *write* it, the guy had the Nobel Prize for Literature. But you were great, you and the other tossers – you got us out, nearly all of us. I heard we were on radio and TV in America!

Ferdinand (*excited*) I'm telling you, the trial stripped the system naked, Jan, and held it up so plain you felt almost sorry for the prosecutor. The absurdity rose and rose till it covered his head and the judge's head . . . but they were trapped in the ritual. Going away from the court afterwards Havel said to me, 'Ferda, from now on being careful seems so . . . petty.'

Ferdinand takes a typed document from his pocket.

So I'm collecting signatures.

Ferdinand gives the document to Jan. 'Charter 77' is a substantial document, about 1,500 words.

It's not a dissident thing, it's a charter – there's Party members who've signed it . . .

Jan gives him a look and sits down to read it to himself.

Exterior – a balloon floats across. There is a leaflet dangling from it.

Milan, suffering in the heat, is waiting for Max.
The exterior scene has its own music, which is cheerful but not loud, like a hurdy-gurdy being played in the street.
A second balloon floats in. Milan grabs hold of the second balloon without difficulty. He detaches the leaflet and glances at it. He casually crumples it.
Max shows up, in summer clothes.

Milan *Ahoj*, Max.

Max *Ahoj, ahoj*. It always gets me . . . As if everyone here's in the navy.

Milan The Czech *navy*? (*Pause.*) You're not at the . . . thing?

Max I get invited to speak, not to listen to brain science. And you. Big fish now.

Milan No, no. Medium size. With a desk.

Max What's the balloon?

Milan Ha! Ask your friends.

Max What friends?

Milan Last night – the friends you skipped the dinner for. (*reproachful*) That was ungrateful, Max. The Philosophy Faculty was under pressure to withdraw your invitation to the conference.

Max Pressure from you?

Milan Tsk, tsk, Max. You don't know who your friends are.

He uncrumples the leaflet.

'Release the prisoners of Charter 77.' (*in jest*) I hope you didn't spend your evening blowing up balloons.

He takes his Party pin from his lapel.

Party pin. Balloon.

He pops the balloon.

Symbolism!

He laughs and replaces the pin.

Max When I left the Party, I didn't go public, you know.

Milan Max, Max . . .

Max There were people in '56 who burned their Party cards in Trafalgar Square. I only told my family. It turned out my son-in-law was sleeping with a woman on his paper, so . . . Whooh! I'm glad Eleanor missed it. You can't imagine what it's like to be this week's carcass for the British press. Esme and her husband are trying to patch things up for the sake of the child, but I entertain some hope that nothing will come of that.

Milan I am so sorry about your wife.

Max Thank you.

Milan So . . . what did you want?

Max You remember Jan. Anyone who gives him a job gets a visit next day and he loses the job. I'm told he's sleeping on friends' floors, living as a beggar. I thought I'd try to do him a good turn.

Milan Max, this is beneath you. Ask me for something worthwhile. Your friend is so unimportant, I'd be ashamed to notice his existence.

Max I have nothing to offer.

Milan Well . . . let me know when you have.

Max Do you know you turned Jan into a Chartist?

Milan No, but hum it to me and I'll pick it up . . .
(*contemptuously*) Chartist! Normal people don't like
Chartists, they like a quiet life, nice flat, a car, a bigger
TV . . . All this 'human rights' is foreigners thinking
they're better than us. Well, they're not better than us.

Max (*more in anger than in sorrow*) But it was you
who called the Charter up from the deep! Is this what
I was keeping the faith for? For some stupid policemen to
make a pig's arse out of a pig's ear? Czechoslovakia was
forgotten. You had it all to yourselves. And simply out
of annoyance, for the sake of venting your spite on a few
drop-outs who were of no danger to you – *no danger at
all* – you made a festival for the Western press to shit all
over the idea that a better way is still possible and looks –
despite everything – looks east to the source.

Milan Max. You know something? You fascinate me.

Max and Milan split and leave.

Jan finishes reading.

Ferdinand We've got over two hundred signatures.

Jan So. What are you going to do with it?

Ferdinand Post it to Husák.

Jan Post it.

Ferdinand With copies to the foreign press.

Jan Though it's not a dissident thing. You're an imbecile.

Ferdinand Okay.

Jan Everything's dissident except shutting up and eating
shit. I wish to Christ I'd learned to play the guitar, but it's
too late now. Have you got a pen?

*Ferdinand gives him a pen. Jan signs, gives the Charter
and the pen back to Ferdinand. He tries the turntable.*

He puts the Beach Boys on it, choosing the track.
Ferdinand watches him uncomfortably.

Ferdinand I'll do tapes for you. I know it's not the same.
I'm really sorry, Jan.

Jan Hey, Ferdo, it's only rock 'n' roll.

The Beach Boys start singing 'Wouldn't It Be Nice'.
Jan starts picking up broken records, dumping them
in a bin.
    Fade to black.

End of Act One.

Act Two

Blackout and 'I Still Haven't Found What I'm Looking For' by U2.

Smash cut to Cambridge. Summer 1987. Garden and interior as before. Night, the interior in near-darkness.

Esme is in the garden, little more than a shadow and a glowing cigarette.

Alice enters the dining area from inside. She is sixteen, and like Esme when young, wearing Esme's old once-red-leather bomber jacket. She turns on a lamp.

Esme Alice?

Alice comes outside.

Alice What are you doing, Mum?

Esme Thinking about something.

Alice No, you're not, you're smoking.

Esme I'm smoking about something.

Alice (*scolds*) Mum.

Esme It's not a hobby, you know. I realised who that man was and my body went, 'Give me a cigarette.'

Alice What man?

Esme That man at the supermarket who said hello.

Alice Who was he, then?

Esme He was the Piper, a beautiful boy as old as music, half-goat and half-god.

Alice Mum, what are you smoking? He was an old baldy on a bike.

Esme When I was your age, I mean. Is this where it's all going if we're lucky? A windy corner by a supermarket, with a plastic bag on the handlebars full of, I don't know, ready-meals and loo paper . . . lumpy faces and thickening bodies in forgettable clothes, going home with the shopping? But we were all beautiful then, blazing with beauty. He played on his pipe and sang to me, and it was like suddenly time didn't leave things behind but kept them together, and everything there ever was was still there, even the dead, coming up as grass or down as rain on the crematorium gardens, so I wasn't really surprised by the Great God Pan getting it together again in my, you know, spaced-out brain.

She steps on her cigarette.

Ashes to ashes anyway.

She picks up the stub and throws it into hiding.

There, look, I've given up, so don't nag me. What did you see? Are you hungry?

Alice The Great God Pan?
No, I had a burger before the cinema, except I didn't go in the end, I just walked around looking to see what I could remember. It's a dump, isn't it, Cambridge?

Esme Some people speak kindly of the college buildings, I believe.

Alice I mean the bus station and Jigsaw and Monsoon an' that.

Esme 'An' that, an' that.'

Alice Virgin was closed . . . When can we go home?

Esme (*irritated*) He's only just got out of hospital! (*Pause.*) Look . . . Grandpa's on crutches, he can't cook, he won't take the rooms the College offered him, he won't have a housekeeper, he's starting to forget things, and altogether he can't be left like this, so how would you feel if I moved back here?

Alice When?

Esme Now. I think I've had Hammersmith, now you've done with Godolfyn.

Alice (*pleased*) Oh. You mean I'd have the flat?

Esme No, you'd be here, with me, of course.

Alice What, I'd have my gap year hanging about Cambridge before starting Cambridge?

Esme You haven't had your results yet.

Alice (*whines in horror*) Mum . . .! What about my friends?

Esme Well, you'd make new friends.

Alice I don't want new friends!

Esme Not so loud. Well, you could live with your dad, I suppose.

Alice There's only one bathroom, and it's in Tottenham! Anyway, with Dad three's a crowd, especially with Busty Babs from the massage parlour.

Esme That's quite enough of that. She's an aroma therapist and I would kill for her tits.

Alice Why can't I have the flat? I'd be all right.

Esme Possibly, but I wouldn't. As it happens, Dad thinks we should sell the flat and divvy it up.

Alice (*cross*) Oh, so you've got it all worked out, the two of you!

Esme Now the paper's upped sticks to Wapping he wants to put his half into one of those dockland conversions . . . and I'd have some spare cash, which would be a novelty.

Alice Oh, right. Good. So Grandpa gets a free housekeeper, Dad gets trendy brick walls with river view, you get a nest egg, and I get stuffed.

Esme (*exasperated, wailing*) Well, what else can I do? I've racked my brains . . .

Alice (*flaming*) Tell Grandpa it's a housekeeper or College or take a chance on being found dead when his phone doesn't answer – *because there are no other options.*

Esme I never thought of that.

Alice Sorted, then.

Alice goes indoors, changes her mind and comes back and hugs Esme. They stay hugging for a while.

Mum.

Esme 'Only one bathroom.'

Alice Well.

Esme If only you'd leave school when people are supposed to, you'd be old enough to be left, or go backpacking somewhere . . .

Alice No, Mum, take it slowly, I'd still be sixteen – waiting for my 'O' level results.

Esme You know what I mean, stop showing me up. (*A dismissive kiss.*) Look in on Grandpa, and don't say anything, leave it to me.

Alice goes back into the interior as Max enters with some difficulty, using crutches. Apart from the leg – he has broken the neck of the femur – he is in good shape for his age.

Alice I was coming to see you. If you're looking for Mum, she's outside.

Max What's forty-three per cent of seventy-five?

Alice Same as seventy-five per cent of forty-three. Thirty-two and a quarter.

Max Thirty-two and a quarter!

Alice Would you like a cup of tea or anything?

Max I would. A small whisky. I can see this is going to work very well, you and Esme moving in.

Alice freezes, then goes out. Esme realises Max has come in. She reacts to go indoors but Max, nimble on his crutches, reaches the frontier.

Esme Pa . . . I said shout.

Max What are you doing in the dark?

Max collapses, groaning, into a garden chair.

Esme I came out to have a . . .

Max That bloody woman's mandate is thirty-two and a quarter per cent!

Esme We can go in.

Max I've just sat down, I'm not moving. Five more years of the haves having it over the have-nots, on a mandate of less than a third of the electorate.

Esme Isn't that good? You wouldn't want *more* people on her side, would you?

Max I'd put you up against Socrates. Your lack of education has made you impregnable.

Esme (*furious*) Go to hell, then, both of you!

Max What's up?

Esme If you don't know, I'm not going to tell you. (*She averts a small weep.*) I'm sick of trying to please everyone and getting patronised for my pains.

Max Never.

Esme Yes, you do. In fact I know about as many things as you do – more, probably – just not career things. I must have been tripping in the water meadows the day they did Socrates. The acid queen of Cambridge High, yeah, that was a joke . . . And now look.

Max Esme . . .

She fails to avert the weep for a moment only.

Esme It's Alice leaving school before I was ready. I'm running out of uses.

Max Alice is a great achievement.

Esme You're doing it. Mum had me *on the side*!

Max Come and sit where I can reach.

Esme scrapes her chair nearer. Max takes her hand.

You're not apologising for not being Eleanor, are you?

Esme (*fiercely*) No! – I do three people's work for charlady pay in a charity shop, even if I still get my sums wrong. But I'm not Eleanor and I'm not Nico either. Nico was with the Velvet Underground. The Velvet Underground was a rock band.

Max I recognised the semiotics.

Esme She had long blonde hair. I had the hair without the band, and two 'O' levels to fall back on. I was grateful to get out of Clarendon Street into a grotty flat in the Milton Road Estate cooking Nigel's dinner with Alice at my breast. The commune got a bit hierarchical.

Max (*interested*) Really? Tell me about that.

Esme (*cross*) No. Stop making everything about *your* thing. I'm talking about, I don't know, being the dog's bollocks at Latin when I was thirteen – which I was.
  Well, I've done that now, so you can.

Max No, I'm justly rebuked.
  Yesterday, standing in the polling station . . . There was no one to vote for. No one. It's not just you.

Esme (*small laugh*) After the drama of getting you in and out of the car?

Max Do you want to know something terrible?

Esme No. What?

Max I thought about voting for Thatcher.

Esme Why?

Max To keep the issues in plain sight. Sharp enough to cut. Draw blood. Widen the gap and rub the workers' faces in it, reward the fat and the smug. Anything to wake the buggers up – anything – *anything* better than five years of amelioration and accommodation calling itself the Party of Labour. But I voted for them. Did you?

Esme I lost the form, the postal thing. Pa – (*She takes the plunge.*) Alice is worried that –

Max Don't worry about her. You'll have to find something to occupy yourself.

Esme I'm not the problem, it's Alice.

Max No, it's you.

Esme (*gives up again*) Let's wait and see when she gets her results. Can we go in?

Max The College doesn't care about her results, it knows what it's getting.

Esme Is that fair?

Max No, but it's just.

He has been easing himself to get up. He relapses.

Give me a minute. Where's that . . . (whisky)?

Esme How is it?

Max Hurts.

Esme starts to get up. Alice enters from indoors with the 'small whisky', and a mug of tea for Esme.

Esme You can have a couple of Neurofen ahead of time, it won't do you any harm.

Max No, I can't . . .

Alice arrives and gives Max the whisky, then the tea to Esme.

Alice (*to Esme, disingenuously*) All done?

Max . . . I'm not allowed the Neurofen with alcohol.

Esme Pa –

Max That's what the doctor said.

Esme No, he didn't! He said you aren't allowed alcohol with the Neurofen.

Max Same thing.

He drinks half the whisky.

Your mother and I have been talking about your gap year.

Alice Oh yes?

Max A gap year in Cambridge is a nonsense. You'd be bored silly.

Alice So, you'll . . .

Max I spoke to the College. You can matriculate in September. You won't be the youngest undergraduate at Cambridge. What do you think? You'll get your degree sooner and have a gap year when you can enjoy it.

Pause.

Alice Yeah, okay. Cool.

Esme (*with relief*) Darling, are you sure?

Max (*handing Alice his empty glass*) Would you oblige me, Alice? It's helping.

Esme (*to Alice*) Don't you!

Alice (*playing along*) My leg's gone to sleep.

Max I'll get it myself, then.

Max feints, Alice takes his glass and a crutch.

Esme Is it all right about your friends?

Alice They're boring.

Alice hobbles indoors using the crutch.

Esme Honestly!

Max There's more of you in her than you think.

Esme Is there? A man at the shops today . . . a bit rough-looking, with his head almost shaved but balding anyway . . . he saw Alice and said, 'Hello, it's you.'

Max Why?

Esme He thought she was me. He used to be in a band, he was quite famous, with wild black hair, you know, a great face, he looked, well, he looked like a rock star, but he blew his mind and the band sort of dropped him . . . and one night, just round that time, before I knew him,

66

before I knew it was him, I saw him in the garden. Just
up there. I had my 'O' level results in my underpants –
the envelope – which I'd, you know, opened but I
thought, 'Well, all in good time' – and I'd gone out to the
Dandelion to see who was playing, and when I came
home late through the garden, he was on the wall
tootling on a pipe, like Pan. (*Pause.*) I wasn't always sure
it happened, like a lot of things. But later he had a solo
album, and . . . well, I went to see him play once, at the
Corn Exchange, in my red-leather bomber jacket I gave
Alice. He was in the support band. It turned out to be the
last gig he ever played, and he was all over the place . . .
The bass player and the drummer tried to stay with him,
they'd find him and he'd lose them again, so they left him
to it but he wouldn't give up, he botched his way on and
on, fudging chords and scowling with his hair falling over
the strings. He'd cut his finger and he was bleeding on the
guitar. It was terrible but somehow great. I got up on the
stage and danced. He looked at me, sort of surprised. He
said, 'Oh, hello. It's you.' He was the Piper.

Blackout and 'Wish You Were Here' by Pink Floyd,
three minutes in.

Smash cut.
    Prague, 1987.
    Exterior open space. Early morning.
    Nigel is waiting, alone, nervous. He has grown up into
a been-around reporter. He has a shoulder-bag.
    Jan arrives. He has a plastic bag containing a record
album, and a paper bag containing bread rolls. He has
weathered the eleven years pretty well.

Jan *Ahoj.*

Nigel Oh . . . hi.

Jan I am Jan.

Nigel (*pause*) Oh, yes?

Jan You are Nigel. Of course.

Nigel Oh.
  'It's my first visit to your beautiful –'

Jan Aaagh! 'Cigarette! Will you give me a cigarette!'

Nigel (*with relief*) Oh, Jesus, what a nightmare! I forgot
the cigarettes, then the shops weren't open, then I stopped
the taxi miles away in case I was being –

Jan (*cheerful, shaking hands*) It's okay! I don't smoke.
Everything is okay. Tell Tomas it is not necessary to
behave like criminals!

Nigel I was worried about getting you into trouble.

Jan Trouble is something else. How is Tomas?

Nigel I don't know him. He's just the guy in London you
call for Czech dissident stuff.

Jan But you are here for Gorbachev, of course?

Nigel Yeah, but our Moscow correspondent is covering
the diplomatic story, he came in ahead of Gorby. I'm
doing dissidents, which basically means queuing up to
interview Havel. So I could use a story if you've got one.

Jan A story?

Nigel (*looking front*) What is all that? I've been
wondering.

Jan The John Lennon wall.

Nigel The John Lennon *wall*?

Jan When Lennon died people started coming here . . . You know, to light candles and play his music . . .

Nigel (*interested*) Really? Are the flowers for Lennon?

Jan (*nods*) The police come and clear everything away and arrest a few people, then it starts again.

Nigel comes forward for a closer look. From nearby there comes the sound of John Lennon singing 'Give Peace a Chance' on a tinny cassette-player.

Nigel Czech hippies! Pictures of him. Has anybody used this?

Jan Is it a story?

Nigel considers, then grimaces.

Nigel It's a piece. But it's not a story.

He goes back, taking a handful of cassettes from his bag.

These are from Esme. She said you probably wouldn't have CDs . . .

Jan (*accepting them*) Thank you! Please tell her thank you. (*slightly surprised*) Uh, Madonna . . . and Queen . . . from Esme? How is she?

Nigel She's okay, fine.

Jan What is she doing now?

Nigel Not a lot. Coping with Alice. Our daughter is starting Cambridge.

Nigel opens his wallet and shows it.

The family brains skipped a generation. That's her.

Jan (*thrown*) With Eleanor?

Nigel With Esme. Alice with Esme.

Jan (*works it out*) Oh. Yes. Can I? (*He looks for a moment.*) She's . . . Thank you. (*abruptly*) This is for her. The Plastic People of the Universe. Live album, very rare, in fact illegal – made from tapes taken out by a tourist.

Nigel (*nervous*) Okay. What happens if I get caught with it?

Jan draws his finger across his throat.

Shit. Really? Okay.

He's ready to go.

Well . . . sorry to get you up so early.

Jan No, I came from work.

He shows a bread roll from his bag.

Still warm.

Nigel (?)

Jan I work in a bakery.

Nigel Right. Okay. It'll have to be Havel.

Jan You don't need Havel. I can tell you Havel. Havel is in despair with the Czech people. When Gorbachev and the beautiful Raisa smile and wave, the Czech people go crazy. They think Gorbachev has come to save them from Husák. When will they ever learn that only they can save themselves?! That's Havel. When we were reformers, the Soviets invaded. Now the Soviets are reformers, they have discovered a deep respect for Czechoslovakia's right to govern itself. Havel can see the joke, it's his business. Why can't President Husák see the joke? Because he knows it's over. He's a realist. Gorbachev got it long ago, he's an economist.

Nigel It's over?

Jan Sure. Gorbachev is a masterpiece. He plays golf, he drinks whisky, his tailor is a reform tailor, he even has a reform wife, and he is a Communist leader! He has discovered the concept of internal political asylum for all. Perestroika!

Nigel Rrright . . . As I say, I'm not doing the think piece. What I need is a story.

Jan There are no stories in Czechoslovakia. We have an arrangement with ourselves not to disturb the appearances. We aim for inertia. We mass-produce banality. We've had no history since '68, only pseudo-history – the newspapers report speeches, ceremonies, anniversaries, announcements of socialism's latest triumph . . . (*nostalgically*) I loved your newspapers.

Nigel Thank you. You're breaking new ground here.

Jan Well, they're human . . . sometimes stupid and barbaric, but with so many papers, all different, there's a correction of the extremes. Here there is only one agent of truth. This is not human – humans disagree with each other.

Nigel Yeah. Right on. Well, I'll get back to the Inter-Continental for breakfast. Good to meet you.

Jan Don't forget . . . (the record).

Nigel (Oh, yeah.)

Jan I was present at this concert, tell her, at Havel's house in the country.

Nigel (*interested*) At Havel's? Recently?

Jan No – before he was in prison.

Nigel (Shit.)

Jan The band had nowhere safe to play, even rehearse, except for a few friends willing to take the risk. After their last concert the police burned down the building.

Nigel (*interested*) When was that?

Jan Oh . . . six years.

Nigel Bollocks.

Jan After that it was more difficult. Emigration, prison . . .

Nigel (*losing interest*) Yeah, shame.

Jan With the police, it was personal against the band. For other bands now we have Rockfest.

Nigel Rock Fest . . . ?

Jan Sure. Even a Communist government wants to be popular. Rock 'n' roll costs nothing so we have rock festival at the Palace of Culture.

Nigel This is better. (*He takes out a notebook.*)

Jan The organisers invited the Plastics to play if they changed their name to PPU. There was argument in the band. Well, it's a question. If you play your music and hide your name, are you making fools of the government or is the government making fools of you? Finally they agreed PPU was not exactly changing their name. They got a girl singer, like Nico, and rehearsed. But the police found out and cut off the electricity.

Nigel has tautened.

Nigel When was this?

Jan Then they were offered to play in a club in Brno if they agreed to be on the poster as 'A Band from Prague'. It was a crisis. Some said yes, some said no. Bad things were said between the band. Terrible things. It finished the Plastics. There is no Plastics now, after twenty years, it's over.

Nigel (*pause*) When was this?

Jan Yesterday.

Nigel (*points his finger at Jan*) I knew you had a dissident story if you tried.

Jan Actually, the Plastic People is not about dissidents.

Nigel It's about dissidents. Trust me.

Jan (*bemused*) Okay.

Nigel Where would I find a Plastic Person?

Jan At Klamovka – it's a pub, in Kosire in the park.

Nigel Can you take me?

Jan (*nods*) I'll call someone. I'll leave you a message.

Nigel Thanks. Which way are you going now?

Jan (*points*) But you can get a taxi on the bridge.

Nigel Fine.

Jan How is Max?

Nigel The old bastard's going to be seventy this year.

Jan Oh . . . yes, October.

Nigel I don't see him. Esme and I aren't together, you know.

Jan Oh. No.

Nigel Yeah. I'll see you later, then.

Nigel walks.

Jan Listen. Maybe you can write about the album. Foreign journalists never mention the music . . . only about being symbols of resistance.

Nigel Yeah . . . that's the story, I'm afraid.

Nigel goes.
Blackout and 'Bring It on Home' by John Lennon
from the 'Anthology' box set.

Smash cut to silence and sunshine. Summer 1990.
At the garden table, Esme is working on something,
with a notebook and textbook. Her summer jacket is on
the back of her chair.
The phone starts ringing in the house. The phone is
answered.

Alice (*off*) Grandpa! Phone!

Alice enters the dining room. Her long blonde hair has
been cropped. She is nineteen now, and grown up by
more than the three years.
The necessary items for six place-settings are
collected randomly on the table. There is a drawer in
the table. Alice takes out six place-mats and starts
laying the table.
Esme completely loses her rag – she jumps up, she
throws her pen down, she tries to tear the book in
two, she throws the book at the table.

Esme Fuck shit sodding buggering bastard *bitch*!

She picks up her chair and is about to hurl it to the
ground when Alice reaches her, smothering her.

Sodding stupid sodding –

Alice It's all right, it's all right! Mum . . .!

Esme Sod the whole thing – and *don't laugh*!

Alice (*lying*) I'm not, I'm not.

Esme sits down, steaming and sulking. Alice looks through the stuff on the table.

So what have we got here?

Hm.

Part One. 'Read the poem carefully –' Oh, not carelessly, then? Right . . . 'Read the poem carefully. One. What metre is Catullus using? Clue, exclamation mark! The poem is Catullus's version of a lyric by the Greek poet Sappho.' Christ, are they giving clues in 'A' level now?

Esme (*snarls*) Just watch it.

Alice Anyway, there's the clue. I wonder if the metre could possibly be . . .?

Esme makes a small sound. Alice cups an ear.

Sorry?

Esme (*mutters*) Sapphic.

Alice Sapphic! So we've done that. 'Two. Scan the poem, clearly marking the feet and the length of each syllable.' As opposed to scanning the poem and not letting on. Okay. Well . . .

She flips through Esme's textbook.

Ah, the Sapphic stanza! Four lines. Tum-ti, tum-ti, tum-ti-ti, tum-ti, tum-ti, with tum-tum as an option in the second and fifth foot – times three.

Esme I know.

Alice Fourth line: tum-ti-ti, tum-ti or tum-tum.

Esme I know!

Alice So the good news is, you never have to decide between a tum-ti-ti and a tum-ti or a tum-tum. It's just a matter of counting the syllables.

Esme Ha! Go on, then. Do the last stanza – and, yes, I did see the elision.

Alice (*glances at the text*) The three elisions, Mum.

Esme Three?

Alice Words ending in 'm' are elided like vowels before a vowel.

Esme Why?

Alice I don't know.

Esme (*furious*) Well, how is anyone supposed to know *that*!

> *Alice shows her the place in the book where it says so.*
> *A young man, Stephen, a few years older than Alice, enters the interior encumbered by four bottles of wine and a tabloid newspaper. He disencumbers himself and sees Alice, who waves him back discreetly. Stephen turns his attention to his newspaper. During this –*

(*with dignity*) Right. Thank you.

Alice (*resuming*) 'Three. Translate the poem into English.' Marks will be deducted for translating into Norwegian. (*translating from the Latin on sight*) 'He seems to me equal to a god, to exceed the gods, that man who, sitting opposite you . . .'

Esme Yes, *thank you*, darling

Alice 'Sees and hears you sweetly laughing –'

Esme *I'm* doing it. How's it coming for the royal visit?

Alice Stephen's here to help.

> *Alice goes inside, 'out of earshot'. Stephen closes the paper and folds it open to a different page. Alice kisses him casually on the mouth.*

Alice You are good. What's Max doing?

Stephen On the phone.

Alice Still?

Stephen What should I . . . ?

Alice Do the table. Six places. I'll find napkins.

Stephen Okay. Oh – no, no, I'm not staying, I'm not family.

Alice Official shag is family, and anyway I want you here for Max – if he gets bored he'll start saying things.

Stephen No – no – she's *your* stepmother.

Alice Are you scared?

Stephen I'll say – have you read her column?

Alice Oh, did you get it?

Stephen Here.

Alice I can't now.

Stephen She's got a photograph.

Alice glances at the photo.

Alice (*laconic*) She looks all right.

Stephen Um, there's a piece about your friend Syd, um, Roger . . .

Alice About the album?

Stephen Not really. I'll keep it for you. He's all right, is he?

Alice Of course he's all right. He's all right when people leave him alone to do his painting and his garden so he doesn't have to talk to them . . .

Max enters. He uses a single stick now.

Alice (*to Max*) Where do you keep the napkins?

Max What's all this?

Alice All what? You haven't forgotten . . .?

Max Oh God.

Alice What have you done?

Max Don't panic. What are you cooking for your dad?

Alice Fish pie.

Max That's a blessing – will it stretch to two extra?

Stephen I'll drop out.

Alice *No*. What do you mean?

Max There's a man come to see me all the way from Prague, and I'm afraid I . . .

Alice But it's meet the wife!

Max It went clear out of my head. Actually, having two extra will stop it turning into the clash of the titans.

Alice (*bristling*) I hope you weren't thinking of having a go at her.

Max I meant you.

Alice slams down a large pepper-mill and marches out in a huff. Max notes Esme, who has remained absorbed.

I said, 'Eleanor wouldn't expect you to go that far.' She became incensed and called me a fool. Apparently it's all to do with a plan she's got to be a lecturer on Swan Hellenic cruises.

Stephen Who's your Czech?

78

*Stephen leaves the paper on the table and starts a
stillborn effort to lay places.*

Max Jan? He teaches philosophy at Charles University . . .
ex-dissident – he was in prison briefly.

Stephen So why isn't he an ambassador, or minister of
something?

Max Now, now. Come upstairs and tell me what the
comrades are doing now that history has ended.

Stephen Can't, I have to lay the table. Why don't you
read the journal, then you'd know.

Max *Marxism Today*? It's not so much the Eurocommunism. In the end it was the mail order gifts thing.
I couldn't take the socks with the little hammers and
sickles on them.

Stephen Well, read the *Morning Star* and keep up with
the tankies.

Max The tankies . . . How the years roll by. Dubcek
is back. Russia agrees to withdraw its garrisons.
Czechoslovakia takes her knickers off to welcome
capitalism. And all that remains of August '68 is a
derisive nickname for the only real Communists left in
the Communist Party. I'm exactly as old as the October
Revolution . . .

Stephen I know, you said.

Max My life would have been neatly encapsulated if I'd
dropped dead in March. From the October Revolution to
the dissolution of the Communist Party of the Soviet
Union. When did it start to go wrong?

Stephen 1917.

*Max's fires are not out. He can still be terrifying. He
swings his stick at Stephen, and brings the stick down
on the table, smashing a plate or two.*

Max You haven't earned the right to condescension! You lilywhite turd, I'll let you know when I can take a joke!

Esme has jumped up and come running.

Esme What's going on?

Stephen It wasn't a joke, Max. I'm sorry if you thought so.

Esme has seen the smashed crockery. She starts gathering it.

Esme What on *earth* –?

Max It seems I've devoted my life to a mistake.

Stephen To *correcting* a mistake.

Esme What are you talking about?!

Stephen (*to Max*) What *I'm* talking about is December 1917, 'The General Instructions on Workers' Control' in reply to the Petrograd Factory Committees –

Esme (*furious*) Oh, for God's sake! You're like a couple of children! –

Max Factory Committees?

Esme – and I won't have it in my house!

Max You anarchist arsewipe!

Esme *That's enough*!

Pause.

Stephen (*meek*) Sorry.

Esme I thought you were coming to help.

Stephen I am helping.

Esme leaves inward with the bits of crockery.

Is it her house?

Max Of course not. It belongs to the College. Jesus. And as for you. Christ almighty. The boy stood on the burning deck arguing the small print of workers' control in the Petrograd Factory Committees.

Stephen You asked me. When Soviet Communism collapsed it was further away from the theory than when it started – so I'd say it went wrong at the beginning.

Max So forget the civil war, the famines, Hitler, American hegemony – it all went wrong when the workers weren't trusted to manage the workplace. You're not an anarchist, you're a utopian. I don't know why you joined.

Stephen I don't know why you left. You've still got the hymn sheet. But it's not Communism if the revolutionary elite is giving the orders and the workers are still taking them. That was the core of the matter, since you asked.

Max Well, it's not the core of the matter for *us*, *now*! The working-class vote could make this a socialist country *permanently*, and they voted in millions for the most reactionary Tory government of modern times. We give them crap. They eat crap, they read crap, they watch crap, they have two weeks in the sun, and they're content. Why aren't they angry? That's the core of the bloody matter!

Stephen Then you should be listening to them instead of despising them for their crap tabloids, crap TV, package holidays – no, really, you hate what's happened to this country – mass culture and yuppy culture, both. The workers have let us down, haven't they? They *jump* to buy their council houses and shares in British Telecom. The Labour Party moved to the left and got trounced – and *you* think the problem is it's not 'left' *enough*. Well, it's over. Marx read his Darwin but he missed it. Capitalism doesn't self-destruct, it adapts. The tankies are in denial, still looking to the melting snowman of organised labour. The Trots can organise revolutionary demos coast to coast, till you realise it's the same fan-base turning up for every gig. We can get the Tories out by modernising. Eurocommunism wins votes.

Max (*angry*) Of course it does. But why call it Communism?

Esme (*entering*) Who're these people you've invited?

Max (*to Esme*) If I said to you 'I'm a Euro-vegetarian, so I'm allowed lamb chops', would you (a) laugh in my face, (b) –

Stephen Fish pie, Max. Not lamb chops, okay? Fish pie.

Esme (*to Stephen*) Alice needs you to do your salad dressing.

Esme moves the paper aside, then notices it.

Oh – is this . . . ?

Stephen (Yes.)

Esme (*like Alice*) She looks all right. 'Candid Candida, the Columnist Who Cuts the Crap . . .' Poor Nigel. 'Candida's Carp' . . . 'Stamps are going up and you know where you can stick it.' Is that grammar?

Stephen I can see you're going to hit it off.

Esme Did you show Alice? Here.

Stephen Actually, hide it somewhere till after. There's a big spread on Syd Barrett, she'll go berserk. It describes him as a vegetable with the wild staring eyes of a frightened animal. That's a bit strange when you think about it.

Esme has found the page.

Esme Oh, God . . .

Stephen They doorstepped him.

Esme He looks sweet. 'A drug-crazed zombie who barks like a dog' . . . Honestly, are they allowed to do that?

Max Who're you talking about?

Stephen Someone Alice knows.

Max What's the matter with him?

Esme Nothing.

Stephen He's a bit turned in on himself, that's all.

Esme stares at Syd's photo.

Esme He used to be so . . .

Alice sticks her head in, shouts for Stephen. Esme closes the paper in response.

Stephen Salad dressing.

Stephen leaves. Esme skims the paper.

Max (*tired*) What is to be done?

Esme Don't worry, I'll see to things now.

She folds the paper back to Candida's picture, pausing over it.

Did you see Nigel's wife's picture?

Max (*leaving*) Don't worry, their byline photos are always years old.

Esme How do you know?

Max It's the sort of thing I know.

Max leaves.
Esme 'hides' the paper in a drawer and goes outside to gather her books. Jan approaches from the garden.

He has a briefcase. He sees Esme. He watches her for a moment. Then she sees him.

Jan *Ahoj.*

Esme Oh my God. Jan.

Jan Yes. Hello.

Esme Jan.

Esme, carrying her stuff, moves to greet him. They manage an awkward combination of cheek kiss and handshake and second cheek.

Jan Max didn't . . . ?

Esme No! No, he didn't. He probably thought he did, but . . . Oh, come inside, why are you in Cambridge?

She leads him indoors and puts her books down.

Jan To see Max. He forgets things now?

Esme A bit.

Jan Seventy . . . three, nearly.

Esme Yes. How long are you . . . ?

Jan Max said for lunch.

Esme Of course, but in Cambridge?

Jan Just to see Max.

Esme When did you talk to him?

Jan Yesterday from Prague . . . and just now from Dr Chamberlain's house.

Esme Sit down a minute. (*Changes her mind.*) No, you want to see Max, of course.

Jan Don't . . . Don't. There's no hurry now.

Jan sits down and puts his briefcase by him.

My first time driving a car in England. Very nice. An adventure. From Stansted.

Esme You rented a car at the airport? Well, of course you did. I worked that out.

Pause.

(*sudden*) Look, there's some wine.

Jan No . . .

Esme Or . . .

Jan No. (*Pause: the books.*) So, what are you . . . ?

Esme Oh, just . . . keeping occupied. Who's Dr Chamberlain?

Jan You know. Lenka.

Esme Oh. Lenka. I didn't . . . She wasn't married in those days.

Jan (*small laugh*) No, of course not. Oh, you mean when . . .

Esme Yes. *What?*

Jan About Max.

Esme That's what I meant.

Jan Lenka told me. Her and Max.

Esme He didn't last.

Jan Nor did Mr Chamberlain, she said.

Esme Oh, so, so you're staying with Lenka?

Jan No. I . . . stopped to see her . . .

Esme Oh – she's the other one to lunch.

Jan She's coming. She has a pupil, extra tuition . . . Plutarch.

Esme So . . . well, you can stay, of course.

Jan No, I have to go back.

Esme (*jumps*) Lunch! – Oh, God – it doesn't matter, it doesn't matter *at all*, but Nigel's just got married – he's my –

Jan Of course. Nigel. With the cassettes.

Esme Yes – that Nigel. He's married a journalist. The fact is they were supposed to go to lunch at Alice's and her boyfriend's, for her to, you know, to meet her new – oh, Alice is my – Nigel's and my –

Jan No, I get it.

Esme Right. But now it's all happening *here*, because she chickened out.

Jan Not enough chicken.

Esme No, she . . . (*prickly*) Are you making fun of me?

Jan No. I'm sorry.

Esme (*pause*) So what's happened?

Jan (?)

Esme Don't tell me, then.

Jan About what?

Esme I don't know. You phone, you get on a plane, you rent a car, you drive to Cambridge, just to see Max, and you drive back to the airport. That's right, isn't it?

Jan Yes. It's really nothing.

Alice comes in with a tray of stuff for the table.

Alice Oh. Hi. Hello.

86

Esme This is Alice. Jan.

Alice Hi.

Jan Yes. Hello.

Esme (*bright*) Some of the cassettes were Alice's.

Jan (*enlightened*) Ah. (*He points his finger at Alice.*) 'Like a Virgin' . . . 'A Kind of Magic' . . .

Alice Oh . . . you're him.

Jan 'Born in the USA'.

Alice finds her ease.

Alice Yeah, that was me, and don't forget 'Now That's What I Call Music' – I gave you good stuff, not like Mum dumping her post-punk techno misery-guts-with-drum-machines she'd gone off.

Esme I thought they were cerebral.

Jan (*serious*) Oh, yes – Kraftwerk, a modernist angst in a period of reaction.

Esme You see? How is the, you know, loaves-and-fishes situation?

Alice FHB. (*to Jan*) I'll see you later. Have you got 'Opel'?

Jan No. What . . .?

Alice There's a new Barrett album – well, not new; out-takes, worth having, though. Mum told me about that night you –

Esme It's got a different take of 'Golden Hair'.

Alice Yeah. Without the overdubs. You should have it.

Alice leaves.

Jan Does Syd Barrett live in Cambridge still?

Esme (*nods*) He's called Roger.

Jan Roger?

Esme It's his name.

Jan It would be wonderful to see him.

Esme Well, you can't, I'm afraid.

Jan I know. I meant, if he just . . . jumped up on the wall. See him.

Esme Alice knows where he lives but you can't go.

Jan Okay.

Esme Don't say I said.

Jan Okay.
    The Rolling Stones are in Prague on Saturday. The Rolling Stones at Strahov . . . Strahov is where the Communists had their big shows. Life has become amazing.

Esme I didn't tell Alice about . . . Only about the wall.

Jan The Great God Pan.

Esme You remember.

Jan Oh yes. Of course.

Esme I saw Syd . . . Roger . . . on his bike one day when I was with Alice, and told her . . . so she bought 'The Madcap Laughs', I only had the vinyl, and next thing . . . well, she's, you know, adopted him – (*Laughs to herself.*) – whether he knows it or not. She protects him.

Jan From what?

Esme Just people bothering him, pilgrims mainly, people who think Pink Floyd have been rubbish since 1968 . . .

Jan laughs.
    Max enters, tipped off by Alice.

Max Jan!

Jan Max. On three legs.

Max Don't be misled, it's my mind that's gone. Did Esme explain? I forgot we had family –

Jan I won't eat.

Max That's not a problem, pilchards are being inserted into the fish pie.

Esme (*alarmed*) I hope not! Get Jan a glass of wine.

    Esme hurries out to save the lunch.

Max Do the wine. I'll have a beer. No glass.

Jan Beer for me also. Thank you.

    Jan deals with the beer.

Max We both look all right. Where's Lenka?

Jan She's coming in half an hour.

    Jan delivers the beer bottle.

Max You need half an hour?

Jan (*laughs*) She has a pupil.

Max Oh, yes. Skol.

Jan Skol.

    They clink bottles and swig.

Max Lenka . . . She told you?

Jan Yes.

Max A little month or ere those shoes were old, hey? Grief doesn't work the way you'd think. It keeps itself to itself, nothing you do has any meaning for it. Doing something is the same as not doing it – grief sucks value out of the world like a bomb sucks out the oxygen. Take the woman to bed; don't take the woman to bed. What's the difference? Stay in; get out . . .

Pause.

Eleanor always spoke up for her. Maybe that was it. (*lightly*) But I don't improve with age, I don't give fair return, I was rude about astrology and the I Ching . . . and Lenka wanted a husband, so she could go home with a return ticket that worked . . .

Jan Max . . .

Max Yes. What's the trouble?

Jan There's no trouble.

Jan opens his briefcase and takes out an ancient cardboard file. He gives the file to Max.

Max (?)

Jan It's your secret police file. *Statni Bezpecnost.*

Max Ah. I did wonder about that. Why have you got it?

Jan A friend gave it to me. Magda. You met her once. She's a lawyer now, working for the parliamentary commission investigating the STB archive.

Max casually opens the folder and glances at the contents.

Max The originals. Some friend. Must be a lot of stuff coming out of the woodwork.

Jan Yes.

Max Well, Jan, I don't read Czech, so you'll have to tell me.

Max gives the folder back.

Jan It's not much, a few meetings with a contact, Milan, a code name, and two documents, from 1968 and 1977.

Max Oh, yes . . . 1968 (*Laughs.*) Somebody in the Cabinet Office . . . dined in Hall one night and got to swanking over the port . . . told us the Sovs were going to bring the hammer down on Dubcek and no two ways about it – he'd seen the minute from the Joint Intelligence Committee. That was a few weeks before the invasion. I thought if I told the Czechs, it might bring Dubcek to his senses.

And 1977, you said. That'll be my briefing paper on the British Left.

Jan gives him a lengthy document.

Is this a translation?

Jan Not a translation, a full abstract. A study of groupings in the Labour government and the Labour Party . . . on Europe, on the Special Relationship, the Cold War, the peace movement . . . Commentary, analysis, predictions . . . also character sketches of certain politicians, apparently very entertaining.

Max Mostly common sense and High Table gossip.

Jan But good low-grade intelligence, it says.

Max's attention is caught as he turns the pages.

Max Why is your name here?

Jan Because it explains – you traded this in exchange for my freedom. In September '77 I was in prison in Ruzyne, sentenced to one year for being a parasite, which is having no work. One day my name was called and two hours later I am standing outside the prison, a parasite once more, but there's a Tatra with three cops waiting for me. 'Get in.' I got in. They said nothing. They drove me to the new bakery in Michle and took me into the office there. The policeman who was in charge said to the boss, 'This man works here now'. Then they drove away, and I worked at the bakery for twelve years.

Max So, good. So this friend of yours, she saw this in my file and, what, she stole it?

Jan Yes. It's a present.

Max A present. And what do you expect me to do with it?

Jan What is that to me?

Max I'll tell you what, Jan. Why don't you take this file and fuck off back to Prague.

Jan (*pause*) Okay.

Max (*angry*) I don't need saving.

Jan Okay. I'm sorry.

Max I've done nothing I'm not prepared to defend. So don't expect me to thank you for telling me different. Have we done?

Jan (*pause*) At Cambridge, being your pupil, invited to the Marxist Philosophers meetings, it was a joy for me . . . this house, your family. Pretending to be a good Communist was ridiculous, but what did I care? I was at Cambridge! They thought they were using me, but I was using them. Mine was the real reality . . . And all they wanted in return from me was . . . a character study, yes, of Max Morrow.

Max Why me?

Jan Hey, Max – an ideological ally and *persona grata* with the ruling class? Sure, why wouldn't they take your measurements? When I read this file I understood how you spoiled my summer vac in '68. How excited they must have been when with no warning you gave them a little plum! I was told not to come home, make myself indispensable . . .

Max What happened when you got home?

Jan They took my albums.

Max Is that all?

Jan I got them back and in return I told them things they already knew. Who was friends of who, you know. They think they're using you, but really you're using them. But finally, in '76, they reminded me who was using who. They smashed up my records. Because, in the end, there are two realities, yours and theirs.

Max Is there a point to this?

Jan I ask your forgiveness.

Max Ah. All right. Go, and sin no more. Is that it?

Max doesn't unbend. It's unsatisfactory, but Jan nods.

Jan What should I do with this?

Max I don't care what you do with it. (*unkindly*) What did you do with yours?

Jan The STB burned many files in the last days of Communism. So it seems I have no file.

Max laughs.

Max Well, then, you didn't have to tell me, did you?

Jan No.

Max gets it, but is not going to go into a swoon about it. He sighs, and unbends enough to oblige Jan with an awkward hug. Jan starts to shake, so Max hugs him tighter.
Blackout, and 'Don't Cry' by Guns 'n' Roses.

Smash cut to:

Lunch for eight at the debris stage, a success by the sound of the babble in which there is some laughter.

Two or more mismatching chairs have been added.

Jan is at one end of the table, next to Lenka. Max is facing Jan at the other end, next to Esme.

There are three conversations going on simultaneously with some energy.

Jan is speaking to Lenka in Czech. She is giving him all her attention, leaning in to catch his words, laughing, happy.

The second conversation is between Nigel, Alice and Stephen.

The third conversation is between Candida, Max and, notionally, Esme, who is not contributing.

Little or nothing intelligible emerges from the babble.

Candida is of an age with Nigel, fortyish, self-made, attractive.

Lenka is still sexy in her early forties.

Jan is telling Lenka, in Czech, about his mother singing and when Jan does the song, in English, his words drop into a hole in the hubbub.

Jan (*in English*) ' . . . but I know we'll meet again . . .'

Lenka laughs.

(*apologising generally*) Sorry. Childhood is a lost country. When I came back it wasn't here.

Stephen When did you come back?

Jan '66 to '68.

Lenka That one is lost, too.

Candida I can't remember the sixties, so I must have been there.

Nigel I thought you weren't born, darling.

Max I was embarrassed by the sixties. It was like opening the wrong door in a highly specialised brothel. To this day there are men in public life who can't look me in the eye because I knew them when they went about dressed like gigantic five-year-olds at a society wedding . . . exchanging bogus wisdom derived from misunderstood Eastern religions.

Nigel I owned a kaftan. Photographs exist.

Lenka Jan had all his hair.

Jan I did. We all had hair. It was our right.

Nigel When I met Esme, she was living in Clarendon Street in a – would you call it a squat or a commune? Esme?

Esme Yes . . .

Nigel I infiltrated to do a story, but – sadly – I went native.

Alice Not sadly. You fell in love with Mum.

Candida Well said.

Max The fifties was the last time liberty opened up as you left your youth behind you. After that, young people started off with more liberty than they knew what to do with . . . but – regrettably – confused it with sexual liberation and the freedom to get high . . . so it all went to waste.

Nigel Right on. Sex, drugs and rock 'n' roll.

Lenka (*protests loudly*) Excuse me, we changed the world.

Candida Yes – what about 1968?

Max What happened in 1968?

Candida Revolution!

Max You'll have to help me. I've got that disease where you can't remember the name of it.

Lenka Candida means the cultural revolution.

Candida No, I don't, I mean the occupations – Paris, the LSE, or in my case, Hornsey College of Art.

Max Oh, the occupations, yes. Do you remember the occupation of '68, Jan?

Alice Grandpa.

Max What?

Alice You know what.

Candida (*smiles at Alice*) Max knows damn well what I'm talking about, and we were all high on bringing down capitalism.

Nigel Bringing down capitalism was Candida's youthful indiscretion.

Max Street theatre.

Candida And ending war. All war, not just Vietnam. I don't know what you mean about the dressing up. I wore a camouflage jacket and combat boots. Oh, I see what you mean. But I also had a Sergeant Pepper coat from Chelsea Girl. No, okay, so we dressed up. So what? We were very political. My boyfriend was a *Black Dwarf* cartoonist.

Jan is taken aback. Lenka explains.

Lenka Newspaper.

Max But Lenka is right. It turned out to be merely a cultural revolution. It left the system in place . . . because, as I could have told you at the time, altering the psyche has no effect on the social structure. You drop out or you fit in. In the end, you fitted in. (*to Esme*) Shove the bottle along.

Candida (*laughs*) And there's me thinking I'm famous for skewering the high and the mighty.

Max (*to Esme*) Bottle.

Stephen pushes a wine bottle past Esme to Max.

Esme What? Yes. Who wants more (coffee) . . . ?

Esme gets up, taking the coffee pot.

Alice (*anxious about her*) Should I . . . ?

Lenka Don't try to put me on your side, Max. 'Make love, not war' was more important than 'Workers of the world unite'.

Jan I agree with Lenka.

Esme glances at Jan and Lenka, and leaves with the coffee pot. Alice follows Esme out, concerned for her.

Alice What are you doing, Mum? I've already filled it.

Lenka (*meanwhile*) Actually, who *owns* the factories doesn't change anything at all.

Stephen (*amused*) Did you get that, Max?

Candida (*scratching the itch*) What do you mean, I fitted in?

Nigel Yes, we're the fourth estate, thank you very much. Good men went to prison to establish the public's right to know.

Max They did, and personally I'd be keeping quiet about them if I were filling half the paper with salacious drivel about celebrities I've never heard of.

Stephen Actually they would have loved it.

Max The proletariat wouldn't follow where Stephen led, so he follows where the proletariat lead.

Alice returns with the coffee pot. She silently offers coffee to Candida and gets a smile.

(*meanwhile, to Candida*) I'll tell you, then. Everything you write is hostage to the market. Your proprietor is in thrall to the consumer. While profits rise, he will reward you for telling lies; while profits fall, he will punish you for telling truth –

Nigel (*explodes*) This is bullshit, Max!

Alice continues her round with the coffee.

Max (*to Candida*) Try skewering your advertisers.

Candida (*cool*) As it happens, my contract says not a word of my column can be changed except for libel.

Max Your contract serves no purpose. Why would you jeopardise your privileges?

Alice Grandpa.

Max (*deliberately mistaking*) No, thank you.

Alice You've upset Mum.

Max How?

Alice How?!

She puts down the coffee pot and goes to her place.

She's gone upstairs anyway. I think she's sickening for something.

Jan (*to Alice*) Is she (all right) . . . ?

Nigel (*pointing to Jan*) Yes – ask *him*!

Max Ask him what?

Nigel Ask him to tell you about truth and lies in your beloved system.

Max I don't need Jan to tell me. Systems don't set out to undermine themselves. Newspapers are part of the system, and truth is relative to that simple fact.

Nigel (*triumphantly*) Thank you!

Max I was talking about your lot.

Nigel (*pressing the point*) Tell him what you said to me in Prague.

Jan What was that?

Nigel Shit, I don't know – you were there. About having lots of different truths being human.

Jan No, I said it was human to disagree about the truth.

Nigel Exactly. That's our system.

Jan But Max is right. How did the propaganda paper and the capitalist press arrive at the same relation to the truth? Because all systems are blood brothers. Changing one system for another is not what the Velvet Revolution was for. We have to begin again with the ordinary meaning of words. Giving new meanings to words is how systems lie to themselves, beginning with the word for themselves – socialism, democracy . . . An invasion becomes fraternal assistance, and a parasite can be someone who is punished by unemployment and punished again for being unemployed – isn't that so, Max?

Max I would have let you stew if Esme had given me any peace.

Lenka Lies didn't start with language . . .

Jan (*to Max*) What do you mean? Esme . . . ?

99

Lenka The first lie was man turning away from his nature.

Candida What about us girls?

Stephen Actually, Candida, did you read your Bonkers Barrett story today?

Candida Mine?

Lenka I read it.

Nigel I suppose you're going to say it's not true.

Stephen Nothing so simple. What it is, is an unrebuttable lie. To anyone who knows, it's an overheated nonsense, apparently written for people with arrested development, and mindlessly cruel, but totally safe, a sort of triumph, really. But the oddest thing about it is that the cruelty and the dishonesty are completely unmotivated, it's just a . . . a kind of *style*. Lenka, why do you buy it?

Lenka It's got the best horoscope.

Max (*to Stephen*) Newspapers are human nature in print, and human nature being what it is, full of cruelty and *superstition*, Lenka –

Nigel (*getting up*) Okay, everybody, thanks very much –

Max – I prefer a *system* where the papers are too boring to do much harm.

Nigel Come on, Candida.

Nigel goes out to get her coat.

Candida I must say goodbye to Alice.

Lenka You think human nature is a beast which must be put in a cage. But it's the cage that makes the animal bad.

Nigel (*returning with Candida's coat*) Goodbye, all.

Max The cage is reason.

Lenka Reason is *your* superstition. Nature is deeper than reason, and stranger.

Max Is this going to be about the I Ching?

Lenka grabs a table knife and advances the length of the table on Max.

Nigel We only came to see Alice. We'll leave you to it.

Alice enters with a newspaper.

Alice Is this your paper, Candida?

Lenka (*stopped*) I think it's mine.

Alice beats the paper to tatters on Candida's shoulders. Nigel pulls Alice away. Alice breaks free and leaves in tears. Stephen follows her. Candida is in shock. Nigel puts his arm round her.

Nigel You're all insane!

He takes Candida out, with a parting shot at Max.

I'll tell you your problem – you've been wrong all your life and now you know it. Come on, darling.

Max, Lenka and Jan gaze at the exeunt. Voices outside, the front door slamming.

Max (*pause*) And it was all going so well.

Max reaches for Lenka's hand, removes the knife, puts her hand to his lips.

It's good to have you back. I was getting boring.

Lenka kisses Max's head.

I asked Lenka to stay.

Jan Oh. Good. To stay?

Max One day at a time, you know.

Lenka It's upset Esme.

Max She doesn't know.

Lenka You didn't ask her?

Max Why? It's my house.

She hits him playfully.

Lenka What's upset her, then?

Jan I don't want to go without . . .

Max drains his wine glass, his mood lowered.

Max There was a place once, a huge country where square-jawed workers swung sledgehammers, and smiling buxom girls with kerchiefs on their heads lifted sheaves of wheat, and there was a lot of singing, and volumes of poetry in editions of a hundred thousand sold out in a day . . . What happened to it?

Jan If pornography was available, the poetry would have sold like poetry in the West. We don't yet understand what we've done.

Max (*grins*) I do.

Jan Tell Esme thank you.

Max Come back and finish your doctorate.

Jan When my mother died I thought of it. Emigration, even.

Max Jan loves England.

Jan (*laughs*) I do!

Lenka You think you do. Don't come back, Jan. This place has lost its nerve. They put something in the water since you were here. It's a democracy of obedience. They're frightened to use their minds in case their minds tell them heresy. They apologise for history. They apologise for good manners. They apologise for difference. It's a contest of apology. You've got your country back. Why would you change it for one that's fucked for fifty years at least?

Esme comes in holding a record album, 'Opel'.

Esme Sorry. I . . . Have they all gone?

Lenka Are you feeling better, Esme?

Esme What do you mean?

She gives Jan the record.

I got you something to take.

Jan Oh . . . Thank you.

Esme In case you, in case you can't get it.

Jan 'Opel'!

Esme (*to Max*) What did you think of her?

Jan puts the record on the table and searches out his briefcase.

Max I was pleasantly surprised.

Esme Really? I hope Alice liked her.

Jan So. Some sunny day.

He shakes hands with Max.

Max Where are you parked?

Jan gestures beyond the garden. He exchanges kisses with Lenka.

Jan I'm glad I saw you, Esme.

Esme Go carefully, then.

They exchange kisses. Jan leaves abruptly by the garden. Lenka starts clearing the table.

Don't . . . don't do that.

Lenka desists at once; an acknowledgement of territory encroached.

Lenka I'm sorry. (*Pause.*) I should have said, Max wants me, has asked me, to stay. Would you mind, Esme?

Max Why should she mind? Shares the burden.

Lenka I won't if it – if you . . .

Esme He forgot to take it.

She picks up the record.

Sorry. What . . .?

Lenka I miss him . . . and Max says he misses me.

Esme Yes. Of course. Of course I don't mind. When did you . . .? (*bewildered*) Do you mean just now, this happened just now?

Lenka He wouldn't get off the phone. I said I'd think about it. (*Laughs.*) But I put a few things in the car.

Esme I saw you were happy. I thought – Oh, Lenka.

Esme embraces Lenka, coughs a laugh.

Where are my . . .?

Esme makes a bee-line for her jacket on the garden chair . . . lights a cigarette, sits down, smokes, stubs the cigarette after two puffs, sits blank.
   Lenka and Max leave the room arm in arm.
   Jan returns to the garden.

Jan *Ahoj.*

Esme Jan. Oh – yes, you left it on the table.

Jan (?)

Esme Did you come back for Syd?

Jan Oh . . . no.

Esme Oh. I came out for a cigarette, then I remembered I don't smoke.

Jan Oh.

Esme I wish I had some grass.

She gestures at the garden wall.

He was beautiful. He was like the guarantee of beauty.

Jan I came to ask you, will you come with me?

Esme Yes.

Jan To Prague.

Esme Of course. Yes. Of course.

Jan Will you come now?

Esme Yes. All right. I'll have to get my passport.

Jan Okay.

Esme It's upstairs.

Jan Okay.

Esme Will you be here when I get back?

Jan Yes.

Esme turns to go indoors, moves, looks back, resumes at speed. Jan picks up Opel and looks at it.
   Blackout.
   'Vera' by Pink Floyd – in entirety:*

'Does anybody here remember Vera Lynn?
Remember how she said that we would meet again?

Vera, Vera, what has become of you?
Does anybody else in here feel the way I do?'

Smash cut to:

Prague exterior, 1990 (Lennon wall).

In the place near the Lennon wall, Esme, in bright, cheap summer clothes, happy behind big sunglasses, has her photograph taken several times by Jan with a cheap camera. The Beatles' 'Rock and Roll Music' plays offstage on a tinny cassette player.

Esme Give us a kiss.

He kisses her briefly, swiftly.

A *proper* kiss.

Jan No. This is Czechoslovakia, you can't behave like in your barbaric country.

He kisses her.

Okay?

Ferdinand arrives at the Lennon wall.

Ferdinand Jan!

He sees Ferdinand coming.

Jan Ferdo!

Elsewhere (Cambridge 1990): Lenka has a pupil.
While Ferdinand joins Jan and they greet each other joyfully in Czech, the Pupil translates Greek in 'sight unseen' Plutarch; Ferdinand continues to speak Czech to Jan (he's telling Jan about his new job in President Havel's office).

Pupil '". . . The third time, Thamous answered the caller, and the caller shouted, 'When you're in earshot of Palodes . . .'"'

Lenka Good.

Pupil '. . . "tell them that Great Pan is dead" . . .'

The Pupil continues unheard, while Jan introduces Ferdinand to Esme.

Jan Ferdinand. He doesn't know English except lyrics.

Ferdinand *Ahoj!*

Esme *Ahoj!*

Ferdinand Ferda!

Esme Esme!

Jan Ferda has a job working in President Havel's office!

Ferdinand launches into a new subject in Czech. The Pupil continues.

Pupil '. . . Thamous was the Egyptian helmsman, not known by name . . .' um, *empleonton* . . .?

Lenka Past participle . . .

Pupil Yes. '. . . to those sailing . . .'

The Pupil and Lenka fade down.
Jan looks troubled.

Esme What is it?

Jan Nothing.

Esme No – tell me.

Ferdinand stands by as Jan starts to explain.

Jan Ferda saw a friend from Plastic People. Now he is in a new band. *Pulnoc.* It means 'midnight'. They're going to America.

Esme What's the matter?

Jan Nothing. Really nothing. These are new times. Who will be rich? Who will be famous?

The Pupil continues.

Pupil '. . . and Thamous in the stern shouted towards the shore – "Great Pan is dead!"'

Magda arrives and calls to Jan.
Lenka and Pupil fade out.

Magda Jan!

Jan Magda!

Jan and Magda embrace.

Jan (*to Magda, in Czech*) This is Esme – the girl from Cambridge.

Magda (*to Esme*) *Ahoj*. Magda.

Esme *Ahoj*. Esme.

Magda (*to Jan, with Czech accent*) Rolling Stones!

Jan But we must eat before the concert.

Continuous: the scene moves to the café tables.
Ferdinand and Magda move to one of the café tables. Jan and Esme sit at the other table. A Waiter arrives.
In Czech, Ferdinand and Magda give their orders to the Waiter.

Magda (*in Czech*) I'll have a beer, nothing to eat.

Ferdinand (*in Czech*) Two beers, and a cheese sandwich for me.

Esme takes the menu from Jan. Jan orders himself a beer.

Esme I'll tell you what I want.

Jan You can't read it.

Esme Can I have anything I want?

Jan Yes.

Esme To start, I want the all-over kissing – and for the main course, I'll have the shagged senseless. I'll let you know about dessert.

Jan (*to the Waiter, in Czech*) Two beers.

Waiter (*in English, Czech accent*) That's four beers and a cheese sandwich, then.

Jan's reaction is deadpan. Esme's reaction is delayed.
The Waiter leaves.

Esme (*catching up*) Did he – didn't he – say that in English?

Jan (*to Esme*) What? No . . . I don't think . . .

Esme He *did*! I don't care! I don't *care*! I don't *care*!

The pre-concert noise starts as on the first track of the Rolling Stones' live album 'No Security'.
Now in the stadium itself, Jan, Esme, Ferdinand and Magda are focused on the distant stage. They jump up when the band appears.
The first guitar chords slash through the crowd noise. The Rolling Stones are seen on the scrim, playing Prague in August 1990. The image fades to black.

The End.

Barrett, Havel and Others: Some Dates

Dates of musical events are in italic type

1967

MARCH
'The Velvet Underground and Nico'.

AUGUST
Pink Floyd, 'The Piper at the Gates of Dawn'.

DECEMBER
Velvet Underground, 'White Light/White Heat'
(June 1968 in UK).

1968

JANUARY
Syd Barrett's last performance with Pink Floyd.

MARCH
Angry demonstrators try to storm the American
Embassy in London after a rally protesting against
the Vietnam War.

MAY
Thousands of students, supported by striking workers,
fight the police in Paris. At the London School of
Economics and other universities and art colleges,
students take over the college buildings. Meanwhile,
Moscow moves Soviet troops to the Czech border,
alarmed by the liberalisation of Czechoslovakia under
the Communist leader Alexander Dubcek.

JUNE
Syd Barrett , 'Jugband Blues' (on Pink Floyd, 'A Saucerful of Secrets').

JULY
Soviet and Czech leaders meet at a frontier village to resolve their differences over the 'Prague Spring'.

AUGUST
20–21 The forces of the Warsaw Pact invade Czechoslovakia.

OCTOBER
Czechoslovakia and USSR sign agreement to allow Soviet troops to remain 'temporarily'.

1969

JANUARY
Czech journalists agree to self-censorship to end their conflict with the government.

JANUARY
16 Jan Palach sets himself on fire in Wenceslas Square, Prague, and dies three days later.

FEBRUARY
Czech Destiny, an exchange between Milan Kundera and Václav Havel.

MARCH
Velvet Underground, 'The Velvet Underground' (April in UK).

APRIL
Dubcek is sacked from the Czech leadership. 'Normalisation' begins in earnest under his replacement, Gustav Husák.

MAY
Czech Central Committee adopts hard-line policies
and begins purges of reformers.

JULY
First man on the Moon.

The Rolling Stones give free concert in Hyde Park for
250,000 people.

NOVEMBER
Syd Barrett, 'Octopus' / 'Golden Hair' (single).

1970

JANUARY
Syd Barrett, 'The Madcap Laughs'.

FEBRUARY
Czech Communist Party announces loyalty checks.

APRIL
The Beatles formally split up.

MAY
Four students shot dead by National Guard at Kent
State University, Ohio.

JUNE
Dubcek expelled from Communist Party.

NOVEMBER
Syd Barrett, 'Barrett'.

1971

MARCH
*'Andy Warhol's Velvet Underground featuring Nico'
(UK).*

1972

JANUARY

Syd Barrett impromptu, King's College Cellar, Cambridge.

FEBRUARY

Syd Barrett impromptus, Dandelion Coffee Bar, Cambridge; Market Square, Cambridge.

24 Syd Barrett's last performance, Corn Exchange, Cambridge.

MARCH

Czech Journalists' Union announces that 40 per cent of journalists have been dismissed since August 1968 for not following the government line.

JUNE

Five burglars arrested in Watergate Building.

1974

Havel spends nine months working in a brewery, the inspiration for *Audience*, his first 'Ferdinand Vanek' play.

1975

FEBRUARY

Margaret Thatcher becomes Tory leader.

APRIL

Havel's 'Letter to Dr Husák'.

1976

JULY AND SEPTEMBER

Seven members of the rock 'n' roll underground

receive prison sentences for spreading anti-socialist
ideas.

SEPTEMBER
Seven Czech writers sign a letter to Heinrich Böll
appealing for solidarity with the rock musicians on
trial.

1977

JANUARY
240 people sign Charter 77, accusing the Czech
government of violating human rights that it had
agreed to uphold by signing the 'Helsinki Agreement'.

AUGUST
Elvis Presley dies.

1978

OCTOBER
The Power of the Powerless by Havel rekindles
'dissident' debate in Czechoslovakia.

1979

MAY
Mrs Thatcher becomes British Prime Minister.

Eleven leading 'Chartists', including Havel, are
arrested. In October, six of them receive prison
sentences of two to five years.

1980

DECEMBER
John Lennon shot dead.

1985

MARCH
Gorbachev becomes Soviet leader.

1987

JANUARY
Gorbachev announces *perestroika* (reconstruction) and greater 'control from below'.

The Czech leadership refuses to publish Gorbachev's *perestroika* speech, despite the fact that Soviet TV is available in Czechoslovakia.

FEBRUARY
Andy Warhol dies.

APRIL
Gorbachev visits Prague.

JUNE
Mrs Thatcher elected for a third term.

DECEMBER
Mrs Thatcher and Gorbachev meet in London.

Husák resigns from Czech party leadership but retains his presidency.

1988

OCTOBER
Syd Barrett, 'Opel'.

1989

NOVEMBER
Fall of Berlin Wall.

Czech Communist leadership resigns.

The USSR and four other Warsaw Pact countries jointly condemn the 1968 invasion of Czechoslovakia.

10 The first non-Communist Czech government for 41 years is sworn in by President Husák, who resigns immediately afterwards.

29 The Federal Assembly, under the re-elected chairman Alexander Dubcek, unanimously elects Václav Havel as President of the Republic.

1990

JANUARY

The Czech government appoints Frank Zappa, the American rock musician, as Czechoslovakia's representative of trade and culture and tourism; later rescinded as 'over-enthusiastic'.

FEBRUARY

President Havel meets Soviet leader Gorbachev in Moscow to agree to the immediate withdrawal of Soviet troops from Czechoslovakia.

AUGUST

The Rolling Stones play in Prague.

2006

JULY

7 *Death of Syd Barrett, six months after his sixtieth birthday.*

SOURCES

Gregory C. Ference, ed., *Chronology of Twentieth-Century Eastern European History* (Gale Research).

Chronicle of the Twentieth Century (Longman).

Julian Palacios, *Lost in the Woods: Syd Barrett and the Pink Floyd* (Boxtree).

Victor Bockris and Gerard Malanga, *Up-Tight: the Velvet Underground Story* (Omnibus Press).

Jan Vladislav, ed., *Václav Havel, or Living in Truth* (Faber and Faber).